MIDLIFE WANDERER:
THE WOMAN RELIGIOUS IN
MIDLIFE TRANSITION

SHEILA M. MURPHY

AFFIRMATION BOOKS

WHITINSVILLE, MASSACHUSETTS

First Edition
Third Printing
© 1983 by Sheila M. Murphy

Two chapters first appeared in *Human Development* in slightly different form. Chapter 3, "Midlife Mourning: The Wake of Youth" was published in Volume 2, Issue 3, Fall 1981 as "Women's Midlife Mourning: The Wake of Youth." Chapter 7, "Midlife Emergence: The Wanderer Returns," appeared in Volume 4, Issue 1, Spring 1983 as "Women Emerging from Midlife Transition." Permission to use this material has been granted by *Human Development*.

Cover design by Rosemary Fay, SND deN

Library of Congress Cataloging in Publication Data

Murphy, Sheila M.
   Midlife wanderer.

   1. Nuns—United States—Psychology.   2. Middle aged women—United States—Psychology.   3. Middle age—Psychological aspects.   I. Title.
BX4220.U6M87   1983   255′.9′0019   83-25806
ISBN 0-89571-018-8

Printed by
Mercantile Printing Company, Worcester, Massachusetts
United States of America

Contents

Dedication

For Mary—

who believes the integration of midlife
is worth the hard coin it demands

Foreword

In October of 1982 I was invited to give the 125th Anniversary Academic Convocation Address at Christ the King Seminary in East Aurora, New York. This academic community gave me as the title of the convocation address "American Church and Priest in the Last Twenty Years of this Century." Obviously I have no more insight into the future than any other human being. However, since it has been my privilege to travel and lecture extensively to priests, religious, and other church ministers, and since I assisted in the foundation of seven therapeutic communities in America and one in England, I reflected that one of the urgent needs for the priest of today is to present a model of health in the ministry of women and men working together. I also made an appeal to take seriously the fact that the priest of today and tomorrow has an obligation to be aware of and to minister to the present situation of women in the Church, and their situation is an ambiguous one.

I continued in that address to state that on the one hand, women exercise many important functions in the Church while, on the other, they are denied all official ministries, ordained and nonordained. The time has come to face seriously this situation and to recognize the validity of ministry for women in the Church. The exigencies of the present time, both in the world at large and in many local churches, demand such a recognition.

There is a growing awareness of the equality of women in all spheres and of their specific roles in human society. The call experienced by many women to dedicate themselves to the service of others in various ministries has had serious repercussions on discussions regarding ministries in the Church. Women are full members of the Church. Discrimination against them exclusively on the basis of sex will deny to the Church the particular gifts and charisms of women. All aptitudes should be recognized by the Church. While the question of the admission of women to ordained priesthood may demand further historical and theological research, their induction into all other ministries has the backing of both theology and tradition. The presence of women in a variety of ministries will also lead to new dimensions of team ministry and to a progressive change in the self-image of the priest.

The Church, therefore, should take steps to prepare both men and women for the change when women will take their rightful place in the ministry of the Church. In the future the Church should also continue the dialogue with the experiences and experiments of women in ministries in other churches.

This book, *Midlife Wanderer: The Woman Religious in Midlife Transition* is by a woman, a doctor of psychology who has had extensive experience with women religious as director of the Center for the Study of Counseling Religious at Walsh College. Sheila M. Murphy's book will not only assist women in general to understand better their midlife transition, but will allow us men to better understand women. There is no humanity without both male and female being very much present to one another during moments of growth. Adult living is difficult work and it is made less difficult and ever so enriching when men and women affirm one another. It is from many women religious, "midlife wanderers," that I have learned so much about my own goodness, the delights of the spiritual life, and the joy of perseverance in ministry. While some of the insights in this book will suggest the need for further investigation and dialogue, *Midlife Wanderer* by Sheila Murphy will encourage our faith and challenge our thought.

By publishing this book, I trust Affirmation Books places itself in the world of dialogue where reflective thought is seen as a necessary ingredient for healthy and holy living.

> Thomas A. Kane, Ph.D., D.P.S.
> Priest, Diocese of Worcester
> Publisher, Affirmation Books
> Whitinsville, Massachusetts

10 October 1983

Preface

I learn by going where I have to go.
—Theodore Roethke

In November 1978, a student in my evening counseling psychology class handed me a copy of Gail Sheehy's *Passages*, saying, "Anyone. who works with adults should read this." Shortly after reading the book, I was invited to dinner by a group of four Dominican sisters, three of whom were in their early forties. To call that evening a conversion experience would be an understatement! Their honest reactions to my comments on *Passages* piqued my curiousity and humbled my youth. Yes, the forties were terrific—peaceful—a convergence of life's vagaries into a meaningful whole. Yes, the late thirties were tumultuous—a kaleidoscope of emotions, dissatisfactions, career questions, vocational crises, sexual longings, and intimacy confusions.

Fascinated by the topic of midlife but aware of my ignorance on the issue, I researched at my college and public libraries and was dismayed at the dearth of information: a smattering of books and articles which tended to be speculative or theoretical rather than concrete and practical. The winter of 1979 had settled in when Jean Mack, S.S.J., asked if I would meet with a "small study group" of her sisters from the Cleveland area to discuss midlife. Despite my protestations that I knew very little about the topic, she insisted that any knowledge was better than none. I consented, only later to realize the immensity of my task: how could I talk with nuns about their midlife turmoils when so little was written about the topic itself—and virtually nothing was addressed to the woman religious' experience of this adult developmental stage? Panic yielded to expediency: if I wanted to know what women religious experienced as part of their growth and development, I would have to ask them. Thus, the study was born.

This three-year investigation of women religious' experiences of the midlife transition, originally undertaken as a scientific endeavor but subsequently purused as an all-consuming personal life interest, developed in four stages: interviews, pilot questionnaire, final questionnaire, and workshop presentations culminating in this book. Each stage added richness, refinement, and clarity while raising more questions.

The first stage, lasting several months, involved a review of the literature and the interviewing of twenty members of an active midwestern community; the interview format was similar to Jean Piaget's *method clinique*, a semistructured procedure in which the answer to one question generates material for the next. "Midlife symptoms" for men and women which appeared in at least two sources were included among the questions explored during the interviews. Additional material for both interviews and questionnaires was provided by the sisters themselves as they responded to questions and discussed their concerns in numerous informal gatherings which emerged as the investigation developed.

Interview questions were based on material from studies conducted on midlife men as well as midlife women for one very pragmatic reason: I did not know where nuns fit! The little bit of research that *had* been conducted with midlife women was concerned chiefly with women in the traditional homemaker role who were struggling to cope with adult children leaving the home, "return to work" problems, sexuality/intimacy concerns, and identity issues. It was obvious that women religious do *not* share the domestic and familial concerns of their married and lay sisters, thus limiting the applicability of many of the research findings. How would the differences between married and religious life-styles affect the experiences of midlife religious and in which areas and to what extent are nuns similar to lay women—both married and single? Midlife research on men, which focuses on career as well as familial concerns, seemed to have something to say to women religious who are professional women pursuing work in a competitive society, but how much?

Sisters between the ages of thirty-five and fifty volunteered approximately two hours each to discuss their personal histories, experiences, and reactions concerning professional development and change, vocational adjustment, intimacy experiences, evolution of spirituality, attitudes toward family and friends, physical changes, and moral/theological issues. Responding to questions about adult developmental life tasks, women religious revealed experiences more androgynous than those of either women or men in general. Although not confronted with growing children and returning to the marketplace, sisters are similar to *women* in general in approximate onset of the midlife transition, emotional experiences of the transition, intimacy/sexuality concerns, and identity issues. Although not confronted in the same way with professional advancement and financial responsibilities, sisters are similar to *men* in general vocational development, career adjustment, and mentoring experiences. Spiritual growth within community, often tinged with a burgeoning awareness of and interest in the feminist movement and its impact on theological outlook and commitment, is an experience *unique* to the religious.

Despite the complexity of the issues explored, identifiable trends in responses emerged and were organized into a pilot questionnaire completed by twenty-three religious between the ages of thirty-five and fifty-five from three different midwestern communities, all engaged in active apostolates. Like the interviews, the questionnaire was primarily open-ended, encouraging participants to elaborate on and clarify their responses. This second stage in the study's development was largely technical, aimed at identifying common experiences.

Data from the pilot questionnaire were then organized into a more detailed, comprehensive eleven-page questionnaire completed by 144 religious between the ages of thirty and sixty from more than fifteen communities in the midwestern, southern, and western United States. Sisters from active as well as contemplative communities voluntarily completed the questionnaire after learning about the study from workshops or friends; no systematic distribution of materials to insure a national random sampling was undertaken. This data-collecting third stage of the investigation generated the fourth and lengthiest stage: continued review of the research, presentation of workshops, and ongoing interviews and discussions with sisters regarding their midlife experiences. The research format—interviews buttressed by the collection of empirical data—has been employed by other behavioral scientists investigating adult development, for example, Daniel Levinson.

This book is the correlation and synthesis of material generated by the four stages of the investigation. While the entire area of midlife transition—and the more specific topic of women religious in midlife transition—awaits more comprehensive and detailed exploration, this presentation provides a framework for understanding and discussing the issues currently believed to be associated with this significant adult developmental marker event. Although the material is presented topically for convenience of organization, this should *not* suggest that the midlife wanderer struggling through transition can neatly compartmentalize, dissect, and cleanly order her upheaval. There are many unanswered questions surrounding the study of midlife transition, but one conclusion is certain: the midlife transition is a pervasive, multifaceted, and often confusing reordering of the *total* person. Perhaps it is this very complexity that has made the midlife experience so impervious to investigation and understanding until recently.

Numbers are always a problem. Levinson worked with 40 men; Sheehy interviewed 115 men and women; this project involved over 200 nuns. The "numbers game" is an omnipresent nemesis to behavioral scientists striving for accuracy when they have access to only a small percentage of the population being investigated. Obviously, to interview *all* sisters in midlife would be the ideal—but a task well beyond the means and energy of any single individual. Until that researcher's dream becomes a possibility, the current presentation is offered with all the cautions inherent in initial, inferential studies; that is, some of the material might be true for most women religious in midlife transition while some might pertain to very few. As more is learned about adult development and as more religious are asked about and feel free to express their feelings about their own experiences, it is likely that some of the material currently considered "definitive" may be rendered incorrect or outdated; other material may be confirmed.

Development does not occur in a vacuum. Sisters contributing to this study have straddled the pre- and post-Vatican II tension of changes in religious life and have experienced a sociocultural upheaval that has challenged traditionally held notions of government, economics, and sex-appropriate behaviors. Their adult experiences will be different from those of their sisters currently in retirement as well as those of their sisters who are just now entering formation. That developmental experiences are both culture- and time-bound, however, does not preclude the necessity of understanding them. Humans are more similar than dissimilar and their developmental processes more predictable than unpredictable. As psychologists, sociologists, and counselors develop a better understanding of adulthood in general, they will be able to understand better the experiences of transition within particular social and temporal environments. All studies of adult development, including this one, are attempts to comprehend and to explore one of the best-kept secrets in the psychology of human development: that there *is* life after twenty-one!

Although over 200 sisters contributed directly to this exploration of midlife, statistics and percentages reported in the various chapters are based on the responses of the 144 women who completed the eleven-page questionnaire, while discussions of issues include input from interviews, the pilot questionnaire, and the final questionnaire; each direct quote is used anonymously with the individual's permission.

No birth is simple or painless. Unfortunately, most of the midwives must go unnamed because they were promised anonymity. You know who you are—you who met with me directly and indirectly, giving precious hours of your busy lives to expose your hopes, hurts, dreams, failures, and loves—to all of you, thank you. I thank you personally and I thank you collectively for all who will learn from you and find encouragement in your experiences and honesty. As you continue to grow in awe and beauty, rest gently knowing you have contributed intrinsically to the development and faith of your sisters; your lives will extend beyond all of us as they encourage our sisters, our daughters, and our friends' daughters to face courageously the challenge to become the unique self that each must become if the earth is to emerge into full fruition.

Some midwives among my sisters I *can* name. To my Dominican sisters, Suzi Repasky, Martha Leyden, Carol Nagi, and Mary Jakubiak: my continuing appreciation, not only for the dinner invitation but also for years of support, humor, tolerance, friendship, and love; may your pursuit of truth set you free. To Jean Mack, S.S.J.: my thanks for your "small study group" of fifty. Ira Progoff once said, "You never know what is coming to bloom," and your "seed" discussion certainly flowered beyond our boldest expectations. To Andre Feulner, S.S.J., and her retreat group: my gratitude for an adrenaline boost that I never really acknowledged to you but which kicked this project from the doldrums into pulsating reality. To Ellen Miller, O.S.F., and your Indianapolis friends: my thanks for invaluable insights and data. To Barbara Ziegler: my appreciation, based on hours of my own such work, for experienced and patient secretarial skills. To Josephine Riffel, O.P.: my thanks for your fine proofreading of Barbara's work.

Editors are special people—the unrecognized facilitators of the writing-publishing process. They remind me of the human heart: they are always there, working hard, and are taken for granted until something goes wrong! Marie Kraus, S.N.D., of Affirmation Books, her editorial readers, and Sean Sammon, F.M.S., international clinical director of the House of Affirmation, deserve special recognition for their belief in this project; they supported, exhorted, and sometimes retorted—always at the right time and with the right degree of force. My debt to them is great!

I want to express a very special gratitude to Mary Jakubiak, O.P. In her love and support, she contributed her own draft-editing and literary skills—her poetic approach to language fleshed out this manuscript with a vibrant sensitivity reflective of her own life attitude and personal spiritual insights. She was "going where [she] had to go" when this study began, learning about midlife in her own person as we both learned about it from the research of this study.

Sheila M. Murphy
Canton, Ohio

Chapter 1
Adult development: The last frontier

I feel that I am in the process of making meaningful decisions, some of which seem critical. I don't feel, however, that my entire being is in crisis.
[age forty-two]

All this "midlife crisis" stuff is just a fad. I never saw my mother go through one and I never saw any of the older sisters go through one. It seems like a convenient excuse for those who can't get their lives in order.
[age forty]

It seems that much of my adolescence was repressed since I entered in high school before working through developmental tasks of identity, sexuality, intimacy. Besides dealing with those issues, I've also experienced the same questioning and breaking out in the area of faith. In some ways my life has exploded in all areas. It has been an exciting time—a time in which I'm wanting and beginning to take responsibility for myself. One of the hardest things for me was to allow myself to admit my immaturity and to allow myself the freedom to explore issues that were *so* scary for me as a religious and someone who has always come off looking very well put together. It has been a very painful time—but very exciting and freeing and I am in touch with some honest power that is honestly me—not just a "put on" to look good.
[age thirty-seven]

Three women religious—three comments on midlife transition—reflect the confusion and lack of agreement surrounding the topic of midlife; their inconsistency is not surprising in light of the limited information available on adult development.

Until recently, adult development and psychology were treated by psychologists as if they did not exist. Textbooks on the psychology of human development, providing comprehensive in-depth studies of physical, emotional, intellectual, social, and moral growth, generally covered periods of growth through adolescence only. This approach led adults entering their twenties to be ambivalent about the "rest" of their lives, fearing decades of static survival while, at the same time, welcoming what they assumed would be a lasting hold on stability, prosperity, and calm. As their lives unfolded and they experienced a reality far different from that suggested in their college textbooks, adults found themselves between the proverbial rock and hard place: they were challenged by changes and questionings for which they were unprepared but which they were reluctant to discuss for fear of appearing "abnormal" or "immature." "After all," they probably reasoned, "if something like this were really significant, I would have learned about it earlier. Since I didn't, I must be unusual." Thus, life confusions and spiritual upheavals were often exacerbated by guilt as midlifers retreated to self-imposed loneliness to avoid the criticisms that they suspected would be forthcoming from their friends if they discovered an "inability to cope." Many of these friends, ironically, would often be going through the same self-doubt while participating in the same masquerade.

The dearth of comprehensive literature on adult psychology was not the result of a deliberate conspiracy on the part of psychologists and life-development experts. Not until this century did people live long enough to experience "a midlife" and the concomitant midlife transition. In 1850, the average life span was forty years; by 1900, this had increased to forty-eight years for men and fifty-one years for women.[1] Today, through improved diet and medical care, American adults can expect to live until their late sixties or beyond. Lengthened life spans create several new "population groups," one of which is midlifers, in much the same way that child labor laws during the Industrial Revolution created the new "population group" known as adolescents.

Academic texts, popular magazines, talk shows, and lectures reflect the burgeoning interest in adult development. Realizing that life is not so stable as they assumed it would be when they graduated from adolescence, adults want to know why they are experiencing what they are experiencing and what, if anything, they can do about it. They demand responses from professionals who, until recently, were able to offer only life span overviews with some suggestions of developmental tasks—quite general in nature—for early, middle, and late adulthood. Empirical research is being developed to substantiate, refute, and refine these general, theoretical statements, but the neophyte status of adult psychology is underscored by the plethora of books, articles, and statements that are often sketchy, contradictory, and disappointing. The problem is further compounded for the woman religious, who does not fit the description of the American homemaker presented in many of the studies.

In approaching the topic of midlife, and its preparatory transition, one seems to find more questions than answers. To what extent is the change physical? emotional? spiritual? Are there things that can be done to prevent these changes? Does childhood have anything to do with the unique experience of midlife, or is it strictly an adult phenomenon? What is the experience of the midlife transition for the woman religious? What can the developing religious expect as she approaches her late thirties and early forties? In what ways does her development parallel that of women in general? In what ways does it parallel that of men? What experiences, if any, are unique to the woman living a celibate community life?

Becoming an adult—the old way

To answer many of these questions, psychologists turned to their traditional theories of personality, hoping therein to discover the makings of the adult. This attempt, though noble and logical in intent, has been futile for several reasons.

First of all, most early theorists, taking their lead from Sigmund Freud, who was the first to develop a comprehensive theory of personality, tended to focus almost exclusively on childhood experiences, speculating that these early encounters with life determined the route of adult development; early experiences superceded adult development in importance. In emphasizing infantile conflicts and childhood confusions to the virtual exclusion of the potential impact of adult experiences, these theorists reduced adulthood to little more than a tedious extension of tensions and problems generated during a developmental period when the individual had little or no control over self or environment. Such fatalistic/deterministic explanations of the human psyche are unacceptable to the intellectual and spiritual palates of the contemporary adult who has been educated to believe that she participates in the ongoing evolution of her self and her person. Traditional theories, it seems, have too little to offer the questioning adult of today; too few are willing to accept the dictum associated with Freud's personality theory that "the child is, indeed, the father of the man."

This dictum highlights a second major limitation of the traditional personality theories: sexism![2] Freud, Alfred Adler, Harry Stack Sullivan, Helene Deutsch, and C. G. Jung were products of their cultures and victims of their cultures' biases, which are reflected in their explanations of personality development.[3] Anne Wilson Schaef, in her book *Women's Reality*, clearly explains how *a* reality—the white, male, middle-class reality—has been wholeheartedly endorsed as *the* reality for centuries.[4] It is a system that affected and still affects economic, spiritual, and psychological understandings.

> Let me explain what I mean by the White Male System. It is the system in which we live, and in it, the power and influence are held by white males. This system did not happen overnight, nor was it the result of the machinations of only a few individuals; we all not only let it occur but participated in its development. Nevertheless, the White Male System is just that: a system. We all live in it, but it is not reality. It is not the way the world is. Unfortunately, some of us do not recognize that it is a system and think it *is* reality or the way the world is.

> The White Male System—and it is important to keep in mind that I am referring to a *system* here and not pointing a finger at specific individuals within it—controls almost every aspect of our culture.... But because it is only a system, it can be clarified, examined, and changed, both from within and without.[5]

Schaef's white male system, sometimes called patriarchy, permeated the speculations of early personality theorists. In this system, the male is normative, implying that anyone or anything that is *not* male is a deviation from the norm and somehow "less than" what "should be." It is not surprising, then, that Freud focused so much on the role of genitals in assessing personality development; after all, the genitals differentiate males, the normative, from females. The male has a penis; the female does not. According to Freud, the female spends her life pining away with penis envy because that is her ticket to mental health, something she can never attain because of her anatomical inferiority! Lest the onus of responsibility for psychological sexism fall solely on Freud's shoulders, it is important to remember that he was simply reflecting a centuries' old nonconscious bias that can be found in the writings of many philosophers and theologians. For example, consider the Church's attitude toward women throughout the years: during the first centuries of the Church, Church Fathers engaged in lengthy debates about women's potential for salvation since only males were made in the image and likeness of God and could be saved. Women's status had not improved much by the Middle Ages when Thomas Aquinas bemoaned the fact that females were "misbegotten males." And now, even in modern times, official Church leaders forbid the ordination of women on the basis of anatomical differences from the person of Jesus.[6]

Schaef's theory is a challenge to the nonconscious sexism of patriarchy. There is a difference between "unconscious" and "nonconscious" ideologies. Unconscious material is material that was once conscious—very much in the individual's awareness—but is now forgotten; it might be resurrected into consciousness through deliberate effort or therapeutic techniques. For example, a woman may be terrified of dogs but not know why; the reason for her fear is unconscious. But, after thinking about her childhood, she remembers that she was frightened by a neighbor's pet boxer who pounced on her unexpectedly when she was four; the reason for her fear is now conscious. Recalling what you had for dinner last night is another example of bringing unconscious material to consciousness.

Nonconscious thinking is more subtle and insidious. It was first conceptualized by Sandra and Daryl Bem, psychologists who applied the term to the unacknowledged bias permeating much of the thinking about women's psychology.[7] Janet Hyde and B. G. Rosenberg define "nonconscious ideologies" in their text *Half the Human Experience*:

> A nonconscious ideology is an ideology (set of ideas) to which we are exposed without being aware of it, either because (1) the ideas are so common and widely accepted that they are not noticed, much as a fish is not aware that it lives in a wet environment, or (2) the ideas are in a form that is subtle and not likely to be noticed or attacked.[8]

Some popular stereotypes generated by nonconscious ideologies include "All blacks are lazy"; "Polish people aren't too bright"; "Women are emotional—men are logical"; "Only men can be priests"; and "Women are the way they are because they lack a penis." Such ideologies are generally exaggerated in jokes and tend to be accepted as eternal verities—*until* they are challenged. The indignant reactions to those who *do* challenge them testify to the strength of such ideas in daily thinking. For example, recall the protests raised against girls who wanted to play Little League baseball ("Girls can't do that. Why? Because they never have before so it wasn't meant to be") or when Theresa Kane, R.S.M., publicly appealed to the pope for women's full participatory involvement in ministry ("She shouldn't have done that. Why? Because nuns don't talk to the pope like that!"). Raising an eyebrow in surprise upon being introduced to a female surgeon or smiling indulgently at a junior high school boy struggling to sew in a home economics class are typical reactions to situations threatening the standard, accepted way that things are "supposed to be." But whoever said that things must be "that" way?

Doctors Bem and Schaef have challenged the nonconscious ideology of sexism in psychological as well as philosophical and theological writings. As a result of their efforts, many beliefs previously thought to be cast in scientific or celestial concrete are being reexamined. Having cherished assumptions questioned is painful, but the resulting opportunities for personal understanding are exhilarating. They allow both women and men greater latitude of awareness and potential for growth.

Patriarchy's nonconscious legacy to psychology, articulated at length by Freud, *did* emphasize the anatomical differences between men and women. If "anatomy is destiny," then the task for psychologists was to determine how a woman's body, her health, and her natural cycles affected her mental health and psychological well-being. This unquestioned assumption, unfortunately, has undergirded most of the research conducted in psychology, particularly research conducted with women.[9] Women were led to believe that their "raging hormones" dictated their emotions and intellect and also that the onset and cessation of menses were the most significant events in their lives. Although it is certainly true that physical and emotional health are interdependent and worthy of study, it is frustrating to realize that women have been studied in this light only. Women who have reflected on their own growth and development suspect that their personalities are dependent upon more than menstrual cycles, childbirth, and hormonal imbalances but are hard-pressed to find substantiation for their intuitions in the professional literature. Women in midlife cannot find much that is helpful in answering their questions when they turn to traditional psychology.

A third limitation of traditional personality theories is their "pathological bias," a negative approach to defining psychological health and adjustment. Most early psychologists and psychiatrists, working primarily with disturbed people, defined mental health as the absence of mental illness. If an individual was *not* phobic, *not* compulsive, *not* hysterical, and so on, then that person must be healthy. Such checklists of personality traits outlined behaviors to be avoided, but did not provide much in terms of qualities to be worked *for*. Abraham Maslow's investigations of self-actualization are a welcome change to this negative approach.[10] Old patterns, however, die hard and slowly; too many people continue to focus on what is wrong with their behaviors and growth rather than on what is right with them.

Becoming an adult—the new way

Contemporary psychologists, alert to the limitations of the earlier theories, have been focusing more attention on adult development and adjustment apart from the traditional systems. Although their approaches are many and varied, they tend to fall into one of two types: stage theories and age theories.

Stage theorists maintain that persons develop (or fail to develop) by successfully (or unsuccessfully) weathering predictable crises in their lives. (Some psychologists use terms like "milestones" or

"marker events" as synonyms for "crises.") These theorists emphasize the experiences themselves more than the time of occurrence.
Examples of marker events or milestones include graduating from
college or graduate school, getting married, making final vows,
entering a life's occupation, having a first child, securing a prestigious
promotion, losing a spouse, or retiring. To encounter, resolve, and
incorporate these experiences leads to greater self-knowledge, wisdom, and integration; to avoid these events for fear of failure or to
fail to resolve them successfully leads to stagnation or retardation in
intrapsychic growth. Because of their orientation, stage theorists
attempt to identify significant life events that characterize various
adult developmental stages, for example, that *most* people get married and begin a family during early adulthood or that *most* people
are coping with adult children in late middle adulthood, and so forth,
so that, armed with this information, they can facilitate growth and
understanding in their adult clients dealing with these problems.

Perhaps the most popular stage theorist today is Erik Erikson, a
psychoanalyst originally trained in the Freudian model who eventually broke from Freud's inner circle because he disagreed with
Freud's emphasis on early childhood experiences. Erikson maintains
that development occurs throughout the life span—not just in childhood—and that growth is dependent on social and cognitive factors
as well as biological ones.[11] According to Erikson, individuals possess tremendous potential for growth and change.

In his description of the eight major stages of development that
occur during the life span, Erikson was the first develomental psychologist to use the term "crisis." He claims that there are periods
during human development in which social, physical, intellectual,
and emotional forces interact in a unique way to produce either
psychological growth or regression. He refers to these "crisis periods" as extended times of personal vulnerability and malleability,
when the personality is modifiable and subject to change. If successful in dealing with a crisis period of vulnerability, the individual will
emerge psychologically and socially stronger, better able to deal with
herself and the world. If unsuccessful, she will be handicapped,
stunted, and less integrated. It is as if the individual were an unfired
clay sculpture that is periodically dampened and warmed so that, in
its softened state, it can be remolded into something infinitely more

beautiful and complete; while softened, however, it can also be twisted into something more hideous, less congruent, or less well-balanced. The softening required for improvement is the vulnerability that can result in something less complete; neither improvement nor destruction can occur without it.

Erikson acknowledged the existence of middle age, without specifying chronological boundaries, when he posited the "generativity versus stagnation" crisis/task for adults. Asserting that adults must shift their focus from establishment and development of the self to that of upcoming generations, Erikson maintains that mature adults must look beyond themselves to the future of society. He does not say precisely when this occurs but suggests sometime between the establishment of a family in early adulthood (the sixth of his eight crises) and preparation for death in late adulthood (the eighth of his crises).

Erikson's theory of personality is much more optimistic than that of Freud; he acknowledges the importance of social, cognitive, and biological forces in the person's psychological development (Freud was exclusively biological) and allows that she can change or modify her personality as she grows (Freud viewed dynamic growth as essentially completed by age five). Religious have found much to assist them in their search for self-understanding by studying Erikson. His material has helped men and women alike. Many contemporary develomental scholars, including James Zullo, F.S.C. (perhaps best known for his tapes entitled "Crisis of the Limits")[12] and Evelyn and James Whitehead (*Christian Life Patterns*),[13] make extensive use of Eriksonian concepts in their presentations of adult developmental psychology. Although Erikson's theory has provided a comprehensive model for understanding adulthood, some women who are sensitive to nonconscious sexism are cautioning against uncritical endorsement of what he has proposed.

Careful reading of Erikson's works, especially *Childhood and Society*, reveals that he nudged personality theory beyond Freud's restrictive focus on infancy and childhood but did not eliminate the nonconscious patriarchal bias. Erikson sees men and women as psychologically different because they are physically different; women have "inner space" because of a womb, whereas men have "projecting, active space" because of a penis. This, he concludes, is why women are fundamentally more passive, nurturing, and home-bound and why men are fundamentally more active, dominating, and involved in the marketplace. "Anatomy is destiny" ideology is again endorsed, and women's supposed innate nurturing passivity (attributable to their possessing wombs, which happen to be interiorly located) is considered the major obstacle to their development in adulthood.

Although Erikson does stress social factors in personality growth, his system still reflects biological determinism, and it should not be surprising that he sees the resolution of the "generativity versus stagnation" crisis in biological terms, that is, in making and growing children for future generations. Many religious who are impressed with Erikson's theory are unaware of this as they repeatedly appeal to his "Eight Ages" (which were originally entitled the "Eight Ages of Man") to explain their personal and religious development in community. True, Erikson's "generativity" can mean more than biological generativity—a point well made by those attempting to apply his concepts to celibates living community life-styles. However, he himself devotes only one paragraph to this rare exception:

> Generativity, then, is primarily the concern in establishing and guiding the next generation, although there are individuals who, through misfortune or because of special and genuine gifts in other directions, do not apply this drive to their own offspring. And indeed, the concept of generativity is meant to include such more popular synonyms as *productivity* and *creativity*, which however, cannot replace it.[14]

To highlight Erikson's nonconscious sexism and biological determinism is not to suggest that his theory is inapplicable to adult female development. On the contrary, Erikson's creative thinking and well-developed theory offer much that is significant to understanding adulthood and will be referred to often throughout this book. These comments illustrate, however, why women in general as well as women religious who are celibate find it so difficult to appreciate and understand their midlife experiences. Even though Erikson's system is helpful, it is ultimately a *male* interpretation of reality reflecting nonconscious sexism rooted in exaggerated anatomical determinism; women who want to understand themselves *a la Erikson* must either adapt themselves to less-then-complete personhood (because of their "inherent" passivity which precludes full adult identity) or else overcome their innate handicaps to become like a man. "Why," women ask, "should we become something other than who we are to understand who we are?"

The dilemma is obvious: if one of the most workable explanations for understanding adulthood is Erikson's stage theory, and if that theory reflects a nonconscious but identifiable sexist ideology, then to what or to whom do women turn for information? As Schaef urges, women must begin to define and trust their own experiences. Such trust is a journey into a foreign land fraught with all the dangers inherent in exploring unknown regions. Women religious must be cautious but bold; they should feel free to employ the tools already available—like Erikson's Eight Ages—but they must be aware of the limitations of their tools and be prepared to fashion some of their own. To the extent that Erikson assists us, we will rely on him to help our midlife wanderer; where he fails us, we will dismiss him with gratitude and regret as we turn to women themselves to help us. Joan Ohanneson encourages women—particularly Christian women—to take the plunge into self-definition in her book *Woman Survivor in the Church* (Ohanneson is speaking to the total self-definition of the Christian woman and not just to the psychological development of the midlife wanderer):

> First, women must set aside time, space, and energy to look at where they have been, where they are, and where they, as Christian women, want to go. And they must do this in the company of other women who, like them, were never consulted on the life or death decisions which affected their minds and their bodies, their hearts and their souls. They must accept the challenge that is involved in the process of self-determination through self-definition; they must accept the fact that while *others may reflect on who they should be, only women can define who they are.*[15]

Endorsing a focus different from that of stage theorists, age theorists measure adult development more by chronological age than by crises or milestones. They acknowledge the existence of significant events but prefer to focus on the age at which these events occur. Perhaps one of the best-known age theorists today is Daniel Levinson, who wrote the landmark text *The Seasons of a Man's Life,* a study of adult growth and development based on his intensive interviewing of forty men.[16] He suggests that adult development be divided into early (twenty to forty years), middle (forty to sixty years), late (sixty to eighty years), and late-late (eighty years and over) adulthood. Within each twenty-year span, he further subdivides the periods into decade-long segments (twenty to thirty, thirty to forty, and so on), indicating that each new decade is heralded by a time of reviewing the accomplishments and experiences of the preceding decade and of planning for the coming one. This reassessment and evaluation last anywhere from two to four years.

During decade-change ruminations, the individual experiences psychological upheaval and restlessness because of the questioning and reviewing undertaken. He (since Levinson worked with men, the masculine pronoun is appropriate) recalls the dreams and ambitions with which he started his twenties or thirties or sixties and tries to determine the extent of his successes or failures in reaching these goals. Mixed emotions—pride and self-doubt—are logical concomitants of his evaluation because he realizes that he has fulfilled some ambitions but has failed in others. Based on the results of his examination, the man must then determine which unmet goals are still worth pursuing and which should or must be abandoned during the next ten years.

Some reassessments, because of the time of their occurrence in the adult life cycle, appear to be more comprehensive and traumatic than others: those that take place in early adulthood (often referred to as the adolescent identity crisis), middle adulthood, and late adulthood. The transition into middle adulthood is just that, a transition *into*—a preparation for—middle adulthood. Without this transition, early adulthood is simply prolonged because the man has failed to accept that a significant part of his life has ended and that he must now prepare for his second major developmental period. As such, the midlife transition is obviously *not* midlife.

Levinson's work, like Erikson's, is most helpful in clarifying some of the ambiguities surrounding adult development; persons who previously thought they were "going crazy" or "losing it" during their late twenties or late thirties have found reassurance in reading Levinson's book. Affirmed in the confusions of their life's journey, they can return to their daily pursuits with renewed confidence and faith.

Despite their value, Levinson's insights are limited when applied to women's adult development. First of all, Levinson's work was done with men; he did not propose to explain female development, and he does not suggest that his findings are applicable to women. To insist that his outline is an adequate description of women's experience is as futile as trying to fit a size ten blouse over size fourteen legs—using different types of measures as if they were interchangeable!

A second major limitation of Levinson's work is his chronological schema for adulthood—the age spans he suggests for developmental periods. Again, Levinson never suggested that his ages were definitive and inflexible, but some who attempt to employ his findings treat them as if they were. When this occurs (and it often happens when people want instant answers to questions, and want those answers to be eternal for the sake of convenience), a tool that can be used to facilitate growth and understanding is unfortunately converted into a bludgeon to condemn persons who, for whatever reasons, have not developed "on schedule," or to explain away problems that might require in-depth study. "So you say you're falling apart? Don't worry! It's nothing! You're forty years old, so it's just your midlife crisis. Stay with it for awhile because it will go away!"

Adult development is more than chronological age. Persons from lower socioeconomic levels, for instance, enter the labor market, start families, and incur chronic illnesses sooner than those from middle and upper socioeconomic levels; they enter their middle years sooner as well. It is evident that a thirty-five-year-old person who has supported a family for fifteen years and who has struggled with poverty and oppression will be much older psychologically and more experienced than a person of the same age who is still being supported by parents while pursuing graduate studies and who has never struggled with difficult decisions and life-and-death situations.[17]

The solution to the problem seems to lie in a "both/and" perspective rather than an "either/or" perspective; adult developmental studies need not be restricted to *either* stage theories *or* age theories, but can be better understood as *both* age *and* stage experiences. Although the onset of adult transitions cannot be determined by chronological age alone, it happens quite regularly that the accumulation of experiences that precipitate a transition culminates around predictable ages in the life span. The underlying assumption of this book is the more eclectic "both/and" perspective.

Is there a midlife crisis?

Admittedly, much of personality theory is limited and many studies are flawed or biased. However, one fact is certain: midlife crisis is here to stay, and women religious are not exempt from the experience. Ninety-one percent of all sisters surveyed responded affirmatively to the question "Do you think there *is* such a thing as a 'midlife crisis'?"

Because all experiences occur within a cultural/temporal context, it is important to understand the sisters who would each willingly invest over two hours of their time completing a detailed questionnaire inquiring into all facets of their adult lives.

Educationally, they are quite an impressive group. The majority, 77 percent, hold at least one master's degree; 6 percent hold doctorates. No study participant reported high school as her highest educational level. Level of education will figure as a significant factor in a person's understanding of adult developmental tasks, especially as it applies to personal understanding of physical changes and career reassessments.

Women religious of today who are between the ages of thirty and sixty most likely entered the convent shortly after high school graduation when they were approximately eighteen years old. Some entered during high school, by way of preparatory programs, and others worked for a year or more before pursuing religious life. Ninety percent of those interviewed entered the convent before they were twenty-one which means that the woman religious who today is between thirty and sixty, who has lived through pre- and post-Vatican II theology, who has witnessed remarkable scientific advancement, and who has been more mobile than any of her predecessors will report a qualitatively different experience from the religious who is now over sixty or the religious who is just entering her thirties.

Asserting that a midlife crisis exists is one thing; determining when it occurs is another. Research on adult males, specifically Levinson's, suggests that the crisis emerges between the ages of forty and fifty with an average onset of approximately forty-three years of age. Is the woman's experiences identical to the man's? It seems not. In her work with both men and women, Barbara Fried discovered that women seem to go through their midlife transition sooner than men do,[18] and her finding supports a trend consistent across all life development tasks: women develop more quickly than men. Females walk, talk, learn to read and write, become pubescent, and enter midlife sooner than males do. For most women, the transition occurs between the ages of thirty-five and forty-five, with an average onset of approximately thirty-eight years of age. Women religious who claim to have experienced a midlife transition identified this age bracket as the time of their crisis, thus substantiating the literature regarding the onset of the transition for women generally. The most commonly reported age bracket for the transition was thirty-five to forty, again substantiating the literature.

Some of those who experienced a midlife transition attempted to describe it:

Reassessment of my purpose in life honed by a realistic look at skills, interests and physical abilities.   [age forty]

Pure hell.   [age thirty-seven]

A real desire to be significant; being severely critical of things which seem to stand in the way of my being.   [age forty-seven]

A feeling that the whole basis of my life was pulled out from under me, a sense of not knowing who I was nor how to relate to others. An intense desire for intimacy and a deep sense of inadequacy.
                                                                       [age thirty-eight]

Moment of depression—feelings of "I've done nothing worthwhile with my life." Does God really care? Is there a God? Is life worth living? God cheated me—made me and then left me without anything! Of what value is religious life?   [age forty-eight]

It is many things: overwhelming, frightening, confusing—the upheaval that it brings permeates every single aspect of life—everything is placed in jeopardy—everything doubted—values, choices, God, ability, vocation.   [age thirty-eight]

The overriding theme is one of totality and pervasiveness. It seems that everything within and outside of the individual shatters to some extent; everything that could be counted on in the past falls apart, shaking her to her very core, leaving her vulnerable, rudderless, and confused. Vocation, profession, prayer life, intimacies, family relationships, and community living are all questioned; nothing is left unaffected.

Although 91 percent of women religious agree that a midlife crisis exists, only 66 percent acknowledged experiencing one. What does this inconsistency, if there is indeed one, suggest?

First, if the average age of onset is thirty-eight, several religious were too young to have experienced the transition. Knowing that something is inevitable and experiencing that inevitability are two different things, a fact noted by many of the women under the age of forty.

Second, the nuns grew up with mothers who, if they had such a thing as a midlife transition, did not talk about it or did not have the vocabulary to talk about it. Likewise, these nuns lived with other religious who, like their mothers, did not talk about midlife transitions if they had experienced them. The concepts of midlife as an identifiable developmental period and midlife transition as an identifiable preparation for that period did not exist even twenty years ago. Lacking information and models with whom they could compare themselves, some women religious were unable to ascertain what, if any, of their life experiences "qualified" as midlife crisis material. They were not alone in their confusions; professionals investigating adult development are not in agreement regarding the existence of the midlife transition and, consequently, are not in agreement regarding "symptoms" signifying the existence of the transition. These inconsistencies reflect the subjectivity underlying much of adult developmental research.[19]

Third, several participants commented on their difficulty with the term "crisis," a word that suggests a singular, catastrophic, devastating event. As such, it did not reflect their unique experiences which, lasting long periods of time, appeared more discomforting and disquieting than singularly catastrophic.

The term "crisis" was first introduced by Erikson; it is his definition that is often invoked by psychologists and theorists discussing major life transitions. For Erikson, a "crisis" is an extended period of personality formation rather than a singular, tumultuous growth spurt which is precipitated by both endogenous (from within) and exogenous (from without) factors; it emerges slowly, irrevocably, and often unnoticed as the individual copes with human growth and development. In the Eriksonian sense, "crisis" is indeed an appropriate word for describing the turmoil and confusion that permeate the midlife preparation—developmental—period. To assume that all people are familiar with Erikson's definition, however, is presumptuous.

Responding to this definitional dilemma, life-span development theorists suggested alternative terms that they hoped would capture the essence of the midlife transition.[20] Because the midlifer in transition questions who she is and what she is about, some theorists suggested the term "midlife identity crisis" because of the similarities between the midlife experience and the adolescent identity crisis experience. A handy reference for some, "midlife identity crisis" is offensive to others because it fails to encompass the intensity, pervasiveness, or seriousness of the midlife transition and to acknowledge that the differences between the midlife and the adolescent transitions are more than academic.

First of all, the adolescent identity crisis has become, for many, a commercial requirement touted by society as a rite of passage from childhood to adulthood. Overstudied, overtheorized, and glamorized to the point of trivialization, it has become a phenomenon that precludes the individual's participation, an "event" rather than a developmental process meaningful to the maturing process. Reacting to the triteness of the term, some midlifers reject the analogy.

Second, the adolescent *knows* that he or she will emerge from the turmoil, confident that mistakes or faulty conclusions can be rectified during seemingly countless years of adulthood, whereas the midlifer does *not* know that she will survive, and even if she does, is not convinced that she will have sufficient time for corrections and modifications.[21]

Third, the adolescent identity crisis has been part of developmental psychology long enough to be understood and appreciated; the midlife transition has not. Secure in the knowledge that parents, teachers, coaches, psychologists, and others can help if necessary, adolescents can embrace their turmoil convinced, to some extent, of its "naturalness" and knowing they can seek assistance. Midlifers, by contrast, are dealing with a recently acknowledged phenomenon, one that is still mysterious to many of the helping professionals to whom they might turn for assistance. Some midlifers question whether it is normal to be so distressed at a time in their lives when everything is supposed to have come together for them, and they are far less open than adolescents about admitting confusion and seeking help.

Although the use of "identity crisis" to describe the transitional experience of midlifers might better characterize the pervasiveness of the turmoil, it conjures up, for some, a weak and sometimes offensive comparison.

"Middlescence," like "midlife identity crisis," is another label used in the attempt to relate the midlife transition to adolescence; it too suffers from all the weaknesses inherent in the previous comparison. Those offended by the connotations of "identity crisis" are equally offended by "middlescence," a not-too-subtle takeoff on "adolescence." Cute to some, it is abhorrent to others. Midlifers are *not* adolescents; their responsibilities, insights, and stresses are quantitatively and qualitatively different; to assume that no more than superficial similarities exist is to misunderstand and misrepresent the midlife experience.

The term used through this book is "midlife transition." *Midlife* identifies the developmental period involved, distinguishing its psychological tasks from those of other developmental transitions, for example, thirties transition or preretirement adjustment. Precisely *when* midlife occurs is dependent upon a combination of chronological age and cumulative life experiences; for women religious today, it seems to emerge around the late thirties.

Transition suggests emergence—change—over time. Neither a singular nor a catastrophic event, the midlife transition is an immersion of an individual's being into an experience of reassessment and growth during which past successes and failures are integrated with current functioning to prepare for a meaningful future. Measured but tumultuous, manageable but unpredictable, it is a growth epoch integral to greater interiority, maturity, and wisdom.

The term "midlife crisis" was employed on the study's questionnaire and in the interviews with the sisters. It could well be that several respondents, who denied experiencing the transition, were in fact *in* transition but were unable to identify it as such because of all the difficulties inherent in the word "crisis." The term "midlife transition," like the experience itself, has emerged as a more precise, accurate, and sensitive description.

Some assumptions are inherent in this book:

1. There is a midlife transition.
2. It is experienced uniquely.
3. It can be empirically validated and described.
4. It reflects the individual's theological, cultural, and educational milieu.

Women religious believe that a midlife transition exists, even if they are not always able to articulate what it is or what it involves. Like women in general, they are exposed to talk shows and popular publications that suggest that a career change, marital upset, or physical deterioration is the totality of the experience. These events may accompany or reflect the transition, but they are not the transition itself; they are symptoms reflecting the more basic, pervasive, and unsettling process of the transition: interiorization.

1. Barbara Fried, *The Middle-Age Crisis,* 2nd ed. (New York: Harper and Row, 1976).
2. Janet Hyde and B. G. Rosenberg, *Half the Human Experience*, 2nd ed. (Lexington, Mass.: D. C. Heath , 1980), especially chap. 1. Other analyses of sexism in early personality theories can be found in Juanita Williams, *Psychology of Women* (New York: W. W. Norton, 1977), especially chaps. 1 and 13.
3. Summaries of these theories can be found in any general text of theories of personality. Particularly detailed presentations can be found in Calvin S. Hall and Gardner Lindzey, *Theories of Personality*, 2nd ed. (New York: John Wiley and Sons, 1970).
4. Anne Schaef, *Women's Reality* (Minneapolis, Minn.: Winston Press, 1981).
5. Ibid., p. 2.

6. Sexism of the Church Fathers, including some quotations from their writings, is critiqued by Madonna Kolbenschlag in her book *Kiss Sleeping Beauty Good-Bye* (New York: Doubleday, 1979), especially chap. 5. More exhaustive discussions of patriarchal bias in theological/philosophical thought can be found in the following: Mary Daly, *The Church and the Second Sex* (New York: Harper Colophon Books, 1968); Daly, *Beyond God the Father: Toward a Philosophy of Women's Liberation* (Boston: Beacon Press, 1973); Daly, *Gyn/Ecology* (Boston: Beacon Press, 1978); Naomi Goldenberg, *Changing of the Gods* (Boston: Beacon Press, 1979); Carol Ochs, *Behind the Sex of God* (Boston: Beacon Press, 1977); Rosemary Ruether, ed., *Religion and Sexism* (New York: Simon and Schuster, 1974); Ruether and Eleanor McLaughlin, *Women of Spirit* (New York: Simon and Schuster, 1979); Ruether, *New Woman, New Earth* (New York: Seabury Press, 1975); Ruether, *To Change the World* (New York: Crossroad Publishing, 1981); Merlin Stone, *When God Was a Woman* (New York: Harcourt Brace Jovanovich, 1976).

7. Sandra Bem and Daryl Bem, "Case Study of Non-Conscious Ideology: Training the Woman to Know Her Place," in Daryl Bem, ed., *Beliefs, Attitudes, and Human Affairs* (Belmont, Cal.: Brooks/Cole, 1970).

8. Hyde and Rosenberg, *Half the Human Experience,* p. 32.

9. Ibid., especially chap. 1.

10. Abraham Maslow, *Motivation and Personality,* 2nd ed. (New York: Harper and Row, 1970). Also see Maslow's *Toward a Psychology of Being,* 2nd ed. (New York: Van Nostrand Reinhold, 1968), and *The Farther Reaches of Human Nature* (New York: Viking Press, 1971). A readable summary of Maslow's thinking can be found in Frank Goble, *The Third Force* (New York: Pocket Books, 1971 [originally published by Grossman Publishers, 1970]).

11. Erik Erikson, *Childhood and Society,* 2nd ed. (New York: W. W. Norton, 1963).

12. James Zullo, *Midlife: Crisis of the Limits* (Kansas City: National Catholic Reporter Publishing, 1977).

13. Evelyn Whitehead and James Whitehead, *Christian Life Patterns* (New York: Doubleday, 1979).

14. Erikson, *Childhood and Society,* p. 267. Italics his; underlining mine.

15. Joan Ohanneson, *Woman Survivor in the Church* (Minneapolis, Minn.: Winston Press, 1980), pp. 186-187. Italics hers.

16. Daniel Levinson, *The Seasons of a Man's Life* (New York: Ballantine Books, 1978). Although she worked with both men and women, Gail Sheehy based her approach on Levinson's work; see Sheehy, *Passages* (New York: E. P. Dutton, 1974 and 1976).

17. Elizabeth Hurlock, *Developmental Psychology,* 5th ed. (New York: McGraw-Hill, 1980), especially chaps. 9, 10, and 11.
18. Fried, *Middle-Age Crisis.*
19. For reviews of the varying conclusions of developmental theorists, see Dorothy Rogers, *The Adult Years* (Englewood Cliffs, N.J.: Prentice-Hall, 1979), especially chap. 6, and Douglas Kimmel, *Adulthood and Aging,* 2nd ed. (New York: John Wiley and Sons, 1980), especially chap. 3.
20. These terms are discussed in Fried, *Middle-Age Crisis.*
21. This insight was suggested by Sr. Jordan Haddad, O.P., at a lecture series on midlife conducted at Our Lady of the Elms, Akron, Ohio, Fall 1979.

Chapter 2
The journey inward: Midlife interiorization

Highly personal, distinctly unique, markedly uncharted, the midlife journey of the soul is a descent into the core of being, into the meaning and essence of life through which the midlife wanderer integrates past experiences with future aspirations to develop a spiritual reason for being which directs the second half of her life. "Dark night of the soul," "the journey inward," "interiorization," "individuation," and "development of the self"—these name the heart of the midlife transition.

The term *individuation*, as well as a description of its process, is credited to psychiatrist Carl G. Jung.[1] Jung, like Erikson, was an active contributor to Freud's inner circle until he eventually defected over irreconcilable ideological differences. Also like Erikson, Jung maintained that development continued throughout the life span. Jung and Erikson differ, however, in the amount of attention devoted to their respective treatments of adult development; Erikson focused on total life development whereas Jung analyzed more comprehensively the span of midlife because of his own experiences during that period.

Jung claimed that midlife is the key time in a person's development. Precipitated by the midlife transition, it is the preparation for the second—and most meaningful—part of an individual's life. In young adulthood, characterized by extroversion, the individual is very other-directed as she selects vocation, career, and a style of doing and being with others. The emphasis of young adulthood, obviously, is in learning the social and technical skills required for fitting into society to receive that society's approbation. Middle adulthood, by contrast, is characterized by introversion, a turning inward, through which the individual reassesses past accomplishments, integrates them into a meaningful identity, and develops a deepened philosophy of life which becomes ultimately a spiritual foundation of personal existence. During this time, the individual strives to establish a personal meaning or ideology, a unified sense of self, without which she never really matures. According to Jung, the individual who fails to meet the challenge of interiorization—individuation—remains forever the "young adult" attempting futilely to find personal meaning in people, activities, and things outside the self. It is only by turning inward, by assessing personal resources and beliefs, that a woman establishes her personal philosophy of life and can identify her unique place in history.

As such, the midlife transition is extremely self-centered; it is an absolutely necessary retreat into the self that must be experienced before the remainder of life can be lived meaningfully. As such, it sometimes disrupts routine functioning. (Jung himself, who had enjoyed a long-standing, intimate relationship with Freud, traces his four years of personal midlife preoccupation to the termination of that friendship; he was unable to teach or maintain his previous level of private psychiatric practice.) Self-absorbed, sorting through ideas and experiences that only she can evaluate from her unique perspective, the midlifer plunges into a reassessment of all aspects of life: physical, spiritual, vocational, social, and emotional; no aspect is left unscrutinized. Interiorization is similar to but distinct from midlife mourning; mourning is grief work with a strong emotional component precipitated by a specific loss, whereas interiorization, which includes emotionality, does not demand a specific precipitating event and extends far beyond mourning as a more incisive philosophical, spiritual experience.

Interiority is triggered by an accumulation of life experiences rather than chronological age and is generally precipitated by some change in the individual's life, either positive or negative. Something happens—or fails to happen—and the individual finds herself unable to resolve the experience with previously established coping techniques. Her equanimity is shattered—she feels inadequate and rootless because she knows the situation in itself is not traumatic enough to warrant the upset, but that something within herself has changed. Gerald O'Collins suggests some type of journey as the precipitating event of the midlife transition, but this is not the only stimulus.[2] Death of a parent, illness in a friend, personal physical changes, a journey, a change of residence, exposure to a summer program, a promotion, or a new assignment can trigger the process.[3] One sister participated in a summer institute for creative problem solving where she had a delightful time meeting new people, living on her own, challenging her intellect, and experiencing affirmation from the other participants. Returning to her local community and her position as a teacher, she was unable to reconcile her summer's excitement and growth with her routine existence which now seemed dull and uneventful in comparison, a conflict that initiated a long, painful questioning of vocation, career, and personal direction. Another sister, an experienced educator and educational administrator, found herself in conflict with the pastor of the parish school of which she was principal. Because of basic ideological differences, she knew she could not operate from his orientation, and was willing to terminate her employment rather than compromise her principles. Parishioners took sides, tensions mounted, and when diocesan officials finally became involved, the woman was forced to take the consequences of her stand. Though supported by her community, she was unsure of the wisdom of her actions, embarrassed about her unemployment, and confused about her future direction. She questioned her career, vocation, integrity, and personal direction. Examples are numerous: one sister traced the onset of her midlife questioning to her appointment as formation directress; another identified a short-lived love affair as the precipitating event of her transition. One woman's election to her community's general chapter stimulated her searching, and another's failure to be elected triggered hers. A forty-five-year-old religious described the onset of interiorization metaphorically when she observed, "Something happens and you realize there aren't any more yellow brick roads."

The questioning inherent in a midlife transition is basically spiritual and philosophical because of the search for values upon which the individual's introspection is based. Jung specifically described the period as a time during which the individual develops a *spiritual* reason for being, without which the second half of life is vacuous and meaningless. All the activities of the first half of life, though necessary, fail to provide ultimate meaning or substance; nothing can be "done," no activity can be "performed," to provide the answer. Personal meaning—personal individuation—must develop in solitude, internally, painfully. If uneducated to the value and predictability of this journey inward, a person might conclude that she is going crazy. In his article "The Crisis of Limits: Midlife Beginnings," James Zullo, F.S.C., describes the transition and offers reassurance of its normalcy:

> In midlife there is often a growing sense of reflection, a tendency to ask more questions about myself and my world. Why am I restless in my ministry? Why do I worry more and more about my aging parents? Why do I get depressed at times? Why am I so confused about my sexuality? Why do I feel so lonely on occasion? Why can't I pray? Why do I seem to know more people who are sick or dying? Why does God seem so silent? From a developmental perspective, these questions indicate the beginnings of the crisis of the limits, and, as such, should be considered on schedule, rather than signs of impending vocational loss or emotional breakdown.[4]

Resolution of polarities

Levinson summarizes the philosophical issues discussed by Jung that must be addressed during the midlife interiorization.[5] Throughout this period, the task is primarily one of resolving the polarities of life, of determining the interdependence of values that had previously been perceived as dichotomous. Establishing a synergistic union of disparate values results in a unified sense of self—an integrated person, symbolized for Jung by the mandala—which is ultimately the goal of life.

Youth/Age

One dichotomy to be resolved is the youth/age polarity. Jung maintained that all people in all cultures, through the collective unconscious, possess a notion of youth, of what it means to be young; this universal image, the *puer* archtype, is characterized by creativity, spontaneity, delight, openness, awe, wonder, and abundant energy as well as irresponsibility, selfishness, ignorance, and self-centeredness.

Jung's archtype for age is *senex* which, like *puer*, is universal via the collective unconscious. Regardless of culture, all persons characterize age as a time of both power and decline, responsibility, insight, rigidity, wisdom, understanding, and knowledge. *Puer* and *senex* each have attractive and unattractive qualities, a fact that often goes unnoticed until midlife.

As the midlifer mulls over her age and experiences, she realizes that although she is no longer young, neither is she old. Attempting to determine just where she falls along the life-span continuum, she discovers that her midlife position gifts her with qualities of both archetypes as she experiences the spontaneity, wonder, and delight of youth tempered by the responsibility, wisdom, and insight of age. She is not purely *either* youth *or* age; she can select and combine qualities of each, ultimately demonstrating and embracing the best of both. This insight, though often painful to reach because of the inherent admission of aging, is freeing and energizing; youth and age are no longer incompatible opposites but interdependent necessities in the unity of life. Each requires the other to modify unsavory aspects while enhancing positive ones. Youth and age *must* be combined for full meaning and richness; youth energizes age while age directs youth. The midlife woman, in an ideal position to embrace both, accepts herself as a rich melding of the two. She retains her spontaneity, now tempered by the wisdom and experience that she lacked earlier in life. She delights in her wonder, knowing that it compensates for her declining ability to seek newness through extensive travel, study, or work. Slowing down, relaxing, seeing things more clearly, she is not really missing anything essential—she is, in fact, seeing so much more that really *is* essential. To persist in her youthful comprehension of youth and age as dichotomous extremes is to remain limited, bound, and handicapped by rigidity, which allows neither youth nor age its full expression in the richness of an integrated life. Successfully resolving the youth/age question for herself, a thirty-nine-year-old high-school teacher explained:

> I used to think I was on the edge of the end, too old and too tired to enjoy the kids anymore. I couldn't keep up [with their pace] and thought I should look for a quieter job outside of teaching. What nonsense! I finally gave myself permission to go at my own pace; I don't *have* to keep up with them and I don't *want* to. Since coming to grips with this, [I] enjoy teaching more than ever and particularly enjoy some of the counseling and administrative work I've gotten into.

Resolution of the youth/age polarity, for some sisters, is impeded by social stereotypes which they must identify and dismiss before they can wholeheartedly embrace the beauty of their midlife selves. Particularly in the United States, commercialization and advertising have glamorized youth—especially youthful women—to the extent that age is implicitly denigrated if not overtly denied. Citing the double standard applied to aging in our culture, that is, "An older man is distinguished looking, more handsome, maturely gray—an older woman is just an older woman," a forty-one-year-old sister commented:

> All my life I feared aging, probably because I grew up believing that I would be a has-been at forty. Well, I reached forty and I certainly didn't *feel* like a has-been! That's when I began to realize how much I had just gone along like a sheep, buying into the stereotypes and allowing them to dictate my self-concept.

Identifying the subtle trap into which she almost fell, this woman, like many other religious, freed herself to resolve the youth/age dichotomy *her* way.

Destruction/Creativity

Personal aging leads to an awareness of destruction as a universal force. Illness, death, destruction, and destructive potential in weapons and industry, the decline of personal physical capacities, and the cyclic destruction in nature coalesce as irrefutable proof to the midlifer that all life seems destined to destroy itself. Realizing that she can do nothing to stem its tide, she is overwhelmed by the perpetual destruction continuing outside of her control. "Why does this happen?" "Where does all this destruction come from?" "What can I do to stop it?"

Attempting to answer these questions, the midlife wanderer realizes that much of the devastation she observes is perpetrated by people—men and women like herself. They build weapons, make decisions, and issue murderous orders. During the early stages of her searching, the midlife woman criticizes a "they" residing somewhere "out there" beyond her—politicians, government and church leaders, multinational corporations, and cold-blooded self-aggrandizers—who seem to have more control over her destiny than she does. As her contemplations deepen, however, she experiences a shift of accusatory focus from the "them out there" to the "me in here." She confronts destructiveness within herself—she has, both deliberately and inadvertently, contributed to the destruction of herself and others through poor decisions, careless living, and irresponsibility. Acceptance of natural destruction, though difficult, is much easier than acceptance of personal destruction. She must own those times when she violated her personal integrity and goals, the times when she compromised her values for the sake of acceptance or promotion, the times she engaged in behaviors that made her less than she was capable of being.

> Healthy guilt is rooted in my assuming responsibility to become what I can be. The belief is that the certain way I should be is one of responding to author my own story. I am responsible for claiming the power for the authorship of my self. The standard, the what, the certain way is simply to be my real self. A healthy guilt would be experienced when I fail to assume the responsibility to answer the call of who I am by developing my true self. I am responsible to continue the creation of my original self. The failure to acknowledge my part in creation is not to assume responsibility for the gift given to me by God.[6]

Some, unable to assume healthy guilt, remain at the level of cataloging their sins. The danger in this type of thinking is that it might perseverate at the self-recrimination stage without progressing to the self-forgiveness stage. This is the distinction between neurotic and existential guilt.[7] In neurotic guilt, an extremely painful awareness of personal culpability, the individual literally wallows in her sinfulness, unable to see beyond what that sinfulness might mean. The guilt becomes its own end—and sometimes, in a perverse way, its own pleasure—because, when neurotically preoccupied with the miserableness of her self and her behavior, the woman's energies are coalesced around self-flagellation (generally mental but sometimes physical) and not around constructive growth. Growth demands change, something requiring considerable hard work. If trapped in the self-defeating mire of neurotic guilt, the individual fails to grow— *cannot* grow—because she is too preoccupied with her misery. Her situation is similar to that of the alcoholic who bemoans the tragedy of her drinking without doing anything about it. Existential guilt, by contrast, is the painful awareness of self-compromise that inhibited or prohibited self-actualization; it is her realization that she was less than she was capable of being. Existential guilt hurts, but it also prods. It encourages the woman to accept herself as a being in the process of becoming and demands that she work toward greater integration and fulfillment.

Facing the ghosts of moments when she deliberately hurt others in anger, revenge, or confusion, she confesses that she contributed in a highly unique manner to the general destruction of life and growth. Destructive wishes as well as behaviors are included in the self-recrimination: "Why did I behave that way? Why did I want that? I thought I would never compromise on that, yet I know I did." Owning and understanding these instances of personal destructiveness, the midlife wanderer wrestles with the responsibility of forgiving herself for these transgressions against self and ultimate actualization.

The midlifer must also accept, understand, and forgive the destruction that others have wrought on her. As she evaluates the damage to her self-esteem, reputation, and pride resulting from decisions and whims of others, though angered and hurt, she moves to forgive with a new knowledge of herself as a codestroyer. She must relinquish the satisfaction of her indignation, surrender her self-sustaining anger, and progress to the more difficult—but life-giving—process of reconciliation. She admits that she has been just as destructive in her own way as they have been in theirs, that she has no grounds for self-righteousness or vindictiveness; just as she forgives herself, so must she forgive others. Forgiveness extends inward and outward toward an impartial healing.

The opposite of destruction is creativity, which can be expressed through material products—novels, paintings, sculptures, or sewing—or through intangibles like relationships, social enterprises, and philosophical understandings. Contemplating the wonder that anything at all could be created in the midst of so much destruction, the midlifer gradually realizes in a new sense that creativity flows from destruction just as destruction flows from creativity. In the same way that nature resurrects itself from winter's death to begin feeding from autumn's lost leaves, the midlifer learns that personal creative growth can flow from her destruction. She learns to gather from the past the seeds of a new season.

Resolution of this polarity between creation and destruction is nothing new to the woman religious, who has long known that life follows death. Nevertheless, "head knowledge" and "gut knowledge" are two different things, and it is not until the midlife transition that she *lives* and *accepts* the maxim of "life after death" which she has contemplated somewhat sophomorically throughout her religious development. She sees with new vision that creativity and destruction are not really dichotomous but circular and interdependent, each requiring the other for full development and expression. More important, creativity and destruction are not forces "out there" to be reckoned with by "them," but processes "in here" to be reconciled by "me." Commented a thirty-nine-year-old sister:

> You know, I've been humbled in the best sense of the word. For years [I was] furious with my community, the church, my superiors—everybody—for my miseries and disappointments. I now realize how I contributed to my own dissatisfaction by living a false self while holding everyone else responsible for me. I can be more honest with me and I can be more honest with them; it was a tough insight to accept, [but I'm] glad I finally saw the light!

Attachment/Separateness

Another polarity to be resolved during the midlife transition is the attachment/separateness polarity, the love-hate tension of relationships. Although he is not specifically addressing midlife issues, John Dunne portrays beautifully the love-hate tension in *The Way of All the Earth*, capturing the pain and exhilaration inherent in the resolution of the tension.[8] This attachment/separateness dichotomy, the watershed issue of relationships, must be resolved if a person is to mature in intrapersonal and interpersonal actualization.

To be attached means to be in relationship with, so even hate for something is an attachment. In midlife, the woman assesses her many attachments—to persons, ideas, things, institutions—and knows that she has become the person she is because of them. Conscious of the considerable time and energy invested in them, she speculates what she would be like if she had employed her strengths otherwise. Although she might be pleased with her relationships and who she has become because of them, she is surprised to discover her pleasure tainted by an irritating awareness of anger and disappointment. "Yes, I am who I am because of you, but I am also not who I might have been because of you." Such contradictions of feeling trigger a love-hate ambivalence that precipitates a thoughtful evaluation of what is truly important to the individual's total actualization, a weighing of everything against its effect on personal worth, meaning, and motivation.

A social being, the midlife woman knows that she needs other people. The paradox is that those very relationships are also impediments that have shaped her, with her permission, into the person she is. Speculations about who she *might* have been apart from those bonds increase. Her first reaction is to demean her relationships, blaming them for demanding so much of her, for usurping her "prime"; at the same time she clings to them for the stability and security she needs to weather her midlife storm. An indignant, "Why did you do this to me?" is juxtaposed with an equally anguished, "Why did I do this to myself?"

Initial projection of blame inevitably yields to guilt and self-questioning: "Why did I worry about that issue? Why did I spend so much time with her? What did I think I was trying to accomplish through that?" Such questioning generates a need for separateness, a time alone to evaluate what is or might be, without interference from or influence of others.

Taking time alone is risky—and socially unsanctioned—behavior. From her earliest days, the little girl is conditioned to develop and maintain relationships; she learns that to be alone means to be unliked, unpopular, unattractive, or unacceptable. To be alone, she is told, is to be somehow personally responsible for her unacceptability; if she finds herself in this dreadful position, she had best do something about it. Men and women alike fear aloneness, but women are more vulnerable to the fear because of social stereotyping which allows little latitude to the female "loner." A man choosing to spend time alone is more likely to be given the benefit of the doubt; he is seen as independent, strong, committed to a cause. His female counterpart is seldom judged as kindly; she is perceived as eccentric, selfish, "stuck-up," or a "poor dear thing nobody likes."

Clark Moustakas offers a term for the irrational but overpowering fear of being alone: loneliness anxiety.[9] Like all phobias, loneliness anxiety causes one to determinedly avoid the feared object or situation—in this case, being alone. Novels, films, and television programs effectively perpetuate the phobia by convincing consumers that aloneness is something akin to cancer, that is, something anyone could contract but would be wise to avoid. The madness is exacerbated by seductive advertising which capitalizes on the individual's fear by suggesting that she can "do" something to avoid this tragic situation: if only she used the right toothpaste or deodorant, purchased the appropriate clothing, or patronized the right establishments, she would never suffer the anguish of aloneness again. The message is insidious for three reasons: (1) it suggests that there is something wrong or abnormal with being alone; (2) it implies that the individual is responsible for her aloneness if it occurs—that she has done this to herself; (3) it offers the facile but false conclusion that something can be "done" to effect a cure. The last completes the illogical circle by assuming that aloneness is, indeed, a disease requiring a cure.

One of the consequences of loneliness anxiety, notes Moustakas, is socially endorsed superficiality of interactions. Because so many are so frantic with fear, they willingly settle for proximity to others rather than work toward being more fully present to others. To risk a meaningful relationship with another is to be vulnerable to potential aloneness—and loneliness—if the other person is away or chooses to terminate the liaison; rather than risk this vulnerability, many prefer to develop wide circles of superficial acquaintances, thus insuring inexhaustible supplies of warm bodies who can be summoned to forestall any aloneness, actual or anticipated.

Moustakas cites another consequence of loneliness anxiety: the inability to experience and grow through what he calls "existential loneliness." Quite different from loneliness anxiety, which is an inordinate fear of being alone, existential loneliness is the human condition. It is the painful but inevitable experience of alienation from self and others; it is the realization that no one—not even my best and most intimate friend—can ever totally know, understand, and appreciate my life in quite the way I do, despite my desire for that interrelatedness. Experiencing existential aloneness is necessary, claims Moustakas, for appreciating the self that each person is; it is a journey to the core of being, including its emptiness, which propels the person back into life and relationships with a deepened, more vibrant appreciation of life. Until she faces herself in the intimate recesses of her soul, the woman does not answer the hard questions of life—who she is, what she is about, and what others mean to her. Existential loneliness is a paradox; it is the realization of ultimate separateness from others that impels the individual to union with others. Those burdened by loneliness anxiety are not capable of this profound insight because they cannot allow themselves the space from others required for its experience; they are too terrified of being alone to allow existential loneliness to lead them into themselves.

Existential loneliness is not pleasant; aloneness and separateness hurt. But it is only through confronting the loneliness, exploring the depths, contemplating the unbridgeable chasm between herself and others, that the midlife wanderer contacts the source of her strength—her God—and her reason for being. Dag Hammarskjöld wrote: "Pray that your loneliness may spur you into finding something to live for, great enough to die for."[10]

Because realization of ultimate aloneness is essential for growth and development, Mary Jakubiak, O.P., suggests that "essential loneliness," rather than "existential loneliness," is a better term for the experience.

> When I hear the word "existential," I think of philosophers and lofty ideas that are somewhat removed from me. But when I think of

"essential," particularly "essential loneliness," I *know* and *feel* the experience. It's real; it's unavoidable; it's in my gut and it hurts.

Sisters unable to relate to "existential loneliness" were indeed able to resonate with Mary's "essential loneliness" as she described it in midlife workshops.

Essential loneliness describes the separateness Jung discusses in the attachment/separateness polarity. Not the extreme separateness of psychotic withdrawal, a total rejection of relationship and interaction, the separateness Jung endorses is the personal withdrawal away from others and into the self that leads to meditation and reverie—the time and space required to assess the self. In her distance, the midlifer wrestles with individuality and uniqueness, realizing that she is ultimately alone. She grew into her present self with and through others, but in the end she is responsible for herself, a self she has grown too distantly comfortable with as she busily established her career and pursued her ideals. Whether she has experienced success or failure, she is disappointed about the relatively negligible effect she has had on the cosmic order—or herself.

"If I had not entered community, would things be different?" "*Now* they tell me I can do something other than teach; if I had been free to change earlier, would I be feeling this way now?" "I love my friends and have grown through my intimacies with them, but what would I be like if I had met different people who were interested in different things?" These questions, unanswerable, raise only more questions. The midlifer questions and questions and questions again until she finally arrives, not at an answer, but at the conclusion that all the people, all the activities, all the involvements are not the issue—*she* is. She is the only person she has, hers is the only life she will live, and following her realization of inevitable mortality, she knows that only she can determine what she and her life are about. In the terror and suffering resulting from these insights, she craves companionship even though she knows that all the relationships, causes, and attachments in the world are insufficient to cancel the essential loneliness she feels. Concluding finally that her ultimate aloneness does not preclude the efforts required to establish ties, she comes full circle, aware now that attachment requires separateness and separateness demands attachment.

Religious learn from their early formation on that change and separateness are inevitable, but learned reality is quite different from lived reality. "Although religious profess to be a death-resurrection people, this perception more frequently reflects rhetoric than reality."[11]

Time to be alone is essential; to deny this is to refuse integration and growth. The midlife woman must see herself alone, experience her aloneness, and accept her uniqueness in all its weakness and glory as she explains for herself, as only she can, why she is who she is. She must develop in that time alone a philosophy of life that incorporates earlier ideas with current knowledge of limitations; she must renew in that time alone her spirituality, discarding ineffective, outmoded explanations (spiritual attachments) and replacing them with deeper, more mature insights. She may emerge from her time alone professing the same beliefs or enjoying the same relationships, but their underpinnings have changed, and they will be qualitatively different because she is different.

Embracing the interdependence of separateness and attachment establishes a new balance in the woman's life; she is more comfortable in her aloneness as well as in her relationships. If alone, she does not question her acceptability to others, and if with others, she does not question her independence; she respects who she is for herself—always.

Masculinity/Femininity

The final, and most controversial, of the polarities to be resolved in midlife is the anima/animus polarity. Jung claimed that there are universal images—archetypes—for masculinity and femininity, and that these images are passed on to all generations in all cultures through the collective unconscious. Jung maintained that the archetype for masculinity, the animus, resides in every female while the archetype for femininity, the anima, resides in every male. The animus is characterized by all those qualities generally associated with culturally prescribed masculine behavior—assertiveness, firmness, strength, and aggressiveness; Logos, the ability to think analytically, is the expression of the animus. Men, by nature, are the embodiment of animus and Logos; women carry both within them but learn through indirect as well as direct childhood training to suppress them. The anima is characterized by qualities generally associated with culturally prescribed female behavior—gentleness, intuition, and understanding; Eros, the ability to make connections, to think convergently rather than divergently, is the expression of the anima. Jung claimed that women, by nature, are the embodiment of anima and Eros; men possess them, but do not learn to express them until midlife because of cultural conditioning and prohibition.

When women do not develop their animus, when they do not learn to live comfortably with it, they externalize it by projecting it onto men, making them the embodiment of all those behaviors, desires, and characteristics that they have been taught to deny in themselves. Likewise, women become for men the embodiment of the anima. The mutual projections result in ignorance, fear, and misunderstandings which inhibit intrapersonal as well as interpersonal growth because half the human experience—the opposite within—is denied. A major task of midlife interiorization is to become acquainted with, to understand, and to embrace the archetype of the opposite sex which resides within. So essential is this task, Jung maintained, that a person can never enter into meaningful relationship with someone of the opposite sex until it is completed. Becoming more knowledgeable about the masculinity within herself, the midlife woman begins to view both sex roles as entities depending one on the other for fruition and complementarity.

Research on middle and late adulthood reveals that men and women increasingly adopt opposite-sex roles as they age; women develop greater outspokenness, assertiveness, and dominance while men cultivate their nurturance, passivity, and gentleness. The freedom accompanying opposite-sex role expression allows the individual to engage in the full gamut of human behaviors while engendering greater comfort and ease with the opposite sex. Acknowledging—living comfortably with—the "opposite within" allows interaction with the "opposite without" that is mutually respectful, mutually appreciative, and mutually free of the fear of manipulation, control, or denigration.

For many, exposure to Jung's anima/animus hypothesis is freeing. They envision a time when antagonism between the sexes will be eliminated, when perfect complementarity will reign, when individuals can develop the "whole self" by accepting the "opposite within." For women especially, Jung offers more hope than Freud—the theorist who lamented that women could never be whole persons because they could never grow a penis! Although Jung may have eliminated some of the negativity surrounding women that Freud introduced, he did not escape the nonconscious sexism of his culture.

Naomi Goldenberg critiques Jung's sexism in her book *Changing of the Gods*.[12] Well educated in Jungian theory, Goldenberg defines flaws in the basic anima/animus conceptualization as well as the nonconscious discrimination of its application.

> Jung is often considered to be an ally of the women's movement because of the high value he placed on "the feminine." It is certainly true that he thought women who exhibited the feminine deserved more respect in Western culture. However, as soon as a woman began to behave in a way that deviated from Jung's feminine archetypes, she was heavily censured.[13]

The first problem with Jung's work, Goldenberg maintains, is his anima/animus archetypes. Jung treats archetypes as universal, innate, incontestable givens in human nature, existing from time immemorial and persisting into eternity. "The archetype becomes the functional equivalent of 'God's will,' which it is quite hopeless and downright immoral to fight."[14] Goldenberg suggests that Jung's anima/animus archetypes are basically descriptions of male and female characteristics as Jung observed them—they reflect *a* reality without questioning *why* that reality exists.

Recent research contradicts Jung's supposition that masculinity and femininity are innate in males and females, respectively. Margaret Mead discovered, for example, that in some societies sex-role reversal is the norm; women exhibit so-called male behaviors and men exhibit so-called female behaviors.[15] If masculinity and femininity were indeed universal and innate, how could these societies come to be? Substantial amounts of research investigating childrearing practices reveal that girls and boys *learn* to behave femininely and masculinely; they are not born knowing these behaviors.[16] This study suggests that if a girl is raised like a boy, she will be quite masculine in her self-expression, and vice versa. Again, Jung's "universal givens" are refuted. In criticizing Jung's approach to archetypes, Goldenberg concludes, "This tendency to generalize about individuals and then to prescribe behavior appropriate to the generalizations is a serious flaw in Jung's work."[17]

Developing the "feminine" exalted by Jung—the behaviors and characteristics indigenous to females—is hazardous to a woman's psychological health. To be feminine, research shows, is to be mentally unhealthy. This finding is the result of a landmark investigation conducted by Inge Broverman and her associates, who asked three different groups of clinicians composed of psychiatrists, psychologists, and social workers to list the characteristics of a socially competent male, a socially competent female, and a socially competent adult, respectively.[18] Three significant findings emerged. First, the qualities of a competent male and a competent adult were virtually identical, thus emphasizing the "male as normative" bias in our culture; to be mentally healthy—socially competent—is to be like a male. A woman who exhibits these behaviors is a healthy adult but an unhealthy woman because she is not demonstrating qualities deemed appropriate for her sex.

Second, socially desirable qualities were assigned to men, socially undesirable qualities to women. "For example, a mature, healthy, socially competent woman is supposed to be more submissive, more excitable in minor crises, have her feelings more easily hurt, and be more conceited about her appearance than a mature, healthy, socially competent man."[19]

Third, assignations of qualities to the three different groups were the same regardless of whether or not the clinician was a man or woman. In other words, female clinicians endorse the same double standard in judging mentally healthy people as male clinicians, thus emphasizing the double-bind dilemma that women seeking therapy generally encounter. To espouse the femininity so highly praised by Jung is, in fact, to endorse qualities resulting in a less-then-mentally-healthy adult. This realization signals the need for caution in wholeheartedly accepting Jung's proclamations of universal, innate, anima/animus archetypes.

Goldenberg identifies inconsistencies in Jung's development of the anima/animus hypothesis. She quotes from his own works to demonstrate that he gave more attention to the animus and Logos in men than to the anima and Eros in women; women were an afterthought. Furthermore, a man who risks development of his anima, expressing characteristics of Eros, is developing into a well-rounded, sensitive person; the woman who attempts to develop her Logos is violating her nature!

> The anima/animus model and its goal of unification works better for men than for women. The model supports stereotyped notions of what masculine and feminine are by adding mystification to guard against change in the social sphere, where women are at a huge disadvantage. In practice, men can keep control of all Logos activities and appropriate just whatever Eros they need from their women as a psychological hobby. Women, on the other hand, are not encouraged to develop Logos. Instead, they are thought of as handicapped by nature in all Logos areas—such as those found at the top of any important profession.[20]

Jungian hypothesizing about anima and animus perpetuates culturally sustained attitudes proclaiming inherent differences between men and women while reinforcing the questionable assumption that males and females are in eternal opposition to one another. The recent upsurge of interest in androgyny studies is an attempt to transcend the masculine/feminine polarity.

"Androgynous," derived from the Greek roots *andro* for man and *gyne* for woman, describes persons exhibiting both masculine and feminine psychological characteristics.[21] Androgynous persons feel free to express *all* human behaviors, and because they are not bound by rigid adherence to socially prescribed sex roles, they have greater latitude of expression and can enter more fully into the total repertoire of human reactions.

Like Jung's anima and animus, androgyny is an appealing solution to the masculine/feminine dilemma; "If only the whole world could learn to be androgynous," we joyfully conclude, "then all the tensions between masculine and feminine would disappear." An appealing solution, for sure, but one that belies an assumption no different from that underlying Jung's anima and animus: that men and women are somehow incomplete in themselves—in opposition to one another—and in need of a complementary melding of the two halves.

More than a transcendence of masculinity/femininity dichotomies, what is needed is a reconceptualization of the human being—what it means to be a person (apart from genitals) and how individuals can strive toward total actualization of their uniqueness. Rather than focusing attention on the socially induced differences between men and women, researchers must begin to consider human completeness, investigating effective methods for attaining this end. To accomplish this task, centuries of patriarchal, white male reality must be abandoned; social systems must change; justice issues must prevail. Such enormous transformations take time, but the survival of humanity is dependent upon them.

Women religious struggle with these problems today. Their responses to questions pertaining to resolution of the anima/animus polarity in midlife reflect their diversity of thinking. Inasmuch as Levinson writes about a male phenomenon developed by a male theorist, the limited applicability of his anima/animus work to women, who experience a different reality, is evident.

It seems that women do indeed reassess their attitudes toward themselves and men in midlife; 79 percent agreed that they had changed their ideas about men, and the most frequently reported age for the ideational shift was the thirty-five-to-forty age bracket. Women religious were not in agreement regarding the nature of their reassessed attitudes; some expressed considerable anger toward men whereas others celebrated a greater sense of peace and harmony with them. These differences seem to reflect the cultural confusion in which they developed.

Women religious today grew up in an environment in which masculinity and femininity were clearly defined and delineated concepts. They strove to develop their femininity—generally prescribed in their rules and constitutions—while interacting with men (usually clerics) in their daily work. Approaching midlife, they have become increasingly aware of themselves as women (through the interiorization process) and are seeking more than a stereotyped understanding of the men with whom they interact. While struggling with the "self-in-relation-to-men" question, they are bombarded by feminist

writings encouraging them to trust their own experiences, to cele-
brate their femaleness, and to question traditionally promulgateed
explanations of the differences between the sexes. A very confusing
situation, indeed! Women religious are not in consensus in their
resolution of the question, but one fact is certain: women religious *do*
rethink the male-female issue in midlife and *are* questioning what
their conclusions mean.

Some sisters' comments reflect a heightened appreciation for men:

Previously thought of men as pretty headstrong and set in their ways.
New chaplain helped me to see that they can be flexible and listen to
new suggestions.   [age thirty-seven]

I have realized that not only is the physical attraction important, but I
find that I am able to give/receive from men on personal/spiritual
levels that I had never allowed myself to do before.
                                                          [age thirty-seven]

I enjoy them more and am not bullied by their overbearing ways.
                                                          [age thirty-nine]

They are not the dominant sex. We can learn lots from each other.
                                                          [age forty]

Most men for me were an unknown quantity, mysterious and distant if
clerics, guarded jealously if married and disinterested if not (school
nuns didn't meet too many bachelors!). Now with my adult groups and
activities, I see men as fellow fragile human beings, each one unique.
                                                          [age forty]

When I felt more sure of myself and felt success in my ministry I was
not so overcome by their authority.   [age forty-four]

I began to appreciate them for bringing the womanliness or femininity
out in me. I enjoyed being with men and was not afraid of relating to or
working with them.   [age fifty]

My apprehension of becoming too close or too forthright has changed
to a great respect, love, sharing in team ministry and enjoying the
complementarity of strengths.   [age fifty-eight]

Other sisters reported anger toward men and the male system in which they function:

> Much more aware of the male-dominated world and church especially. See their faults and limitations more. [age thirty-six]

> Just recently I have been angry with men. [age forty-three]

> I have become more negative in my attitude. Perhaps the feminist movement has helped. [age forty-seven]

> They are not so awesome and grand; many I know are weak and petty and, may I say, inferior to most of the women I know.
> [age forty-eight]

> Became very much aware of male power in the last fifteen years and resent it, especially within the Church. Tired of taking second place to idiocy. [age fifty-seven]

Whatever her conclusions about men, the midlife wanderer wrestles with the question of her personal identity—individuation—and struggles to integrate her conclusions with her daily interactions. Whether she is appreciative of men or angry with them, she demonstrates a greater acceptance of self when relating with them.

For Jung, the self is the goal of the integrated person. Through the work of interiorization, the individual fashions the person she is— and her reasons for being that person—in the privacy of her soul. The internal struggle with the spiritual and philosophical questions of life is the heart of the midlife transition. It is highly personal and intrinsically contemplative, requiring time, distance, and silence. It might be assumed that women religious, who have woven the very fabric of their lives out of prayer, contemplation, and spirituality, would survive midlife interiority with minimal disruption to their overall functioning. This seems not to be the case.

When the well runs dry at midlife

Dedication to a life of prayer does not constitute a guaranteed exemption from or minimalization of the spiritual upheavals of interiorization. Slightly more than half of the survey participants, 56 percent, experienced some sort of crisis of faith. The ages reported reveal a bimodal distribution of onset indicating that faith issues emerge significantly during two major developmental periods: early adulthood and midlife transition. Even those who questioned and struggled during their novitiate and prior to final vows again experienced upheaval during their midlife transition, suggesting that faith issues are not resolved through a singular confrontation.

Further data make it even more evident that women religious are not exempt from the spiritual upheaval characteristic of the midlife transition. Eighty-two percent experienced an extended dry period in prayer, with 51 percent indicating the years between thirty-five and forty-five as their "desert time."

Sisters' comments about their spiritual growth and prayer lives indicate a shift from satisfaction with rote, articulated prayer to an insistent craving for quiet, contemplative prayer. Reflecting the maturing process as an evolution toward "wholeness," spiritual growth parallels psychological growth in a movement from "doing" to "being."

> From twenty to thirty, I used the Ignatian meditations and the divine office: both somewhat mechanical. From thirty-one to thirty-five I spent very little time in personal prayer although I was beginning to experience a more contemplative response to God. From thirty-six to forty, my prayer became more incarnational/contemplative/celebrative.   [age thirty-nine]

> From twenty to thirty, rather formalized. From thirty-one to thirty-five, sporadic, distracted. Ministry was more important than prayer. From thirty-six to forty, more integrated—more often in small groups; more peacefilled.   [age forty]

> I was *very* pious in my twenties; prayed office regularly, attended daily Mass. I started reading in women's studies about three years ago and have been unable to pray "conventional" male-dominated prayers since. *Very* upset with self and community for doing so little exploration in alternate prayer forms.   [age thirty-eight]

> In my twenties, I prayed with the attitude, "I'm going to be *perfect* at this." I moved through indifference to a crisis of faith. Now I experience God with me, loving me, calling me to deeper union with Him.

I'm beginning to become more aware of Him with me throughout the day and that all is a prayer. [age forty-five]

From twenty to thirty it was more "saying" than praying. In my early thirties, I gradually moved into meditation. From thirty-six on, a quiet sitting with the Lord, waiting for His word, occasionally speaking to Him. During the day a quick thought of God, recommitting myself to Him. Occasional short periods (one or two days) of dryness. [age fifty-three]

I suspected in my teens that God was, to some extent, me. Afraid to think that through for fear of its "heretical" consequences, I went along with "sage advice," praying in the prescribed ways. Now I have finished with the rote, ritual, and prescribed and have explored my "God-in-me intuitions" and feel much more grounded in reality. While I was finished with forms by mid-life, I summoned up the honesty to say so only after the turmoils of my early forties. [age forty-eight]

Their growth patterns can be explained as developmental progress through the faith stages proposed by Jim Fowler, who based his work on that of Piaget and Lawrence Kohlberg.[22] He theorizes that faith development occurs in a hierarchical progression through six invariant stages which reflect the individual's psychological and social self-awareness. A simple description of faith progress would be to say that the individual moves from a world/faith view that is primarily egocentric (comparable to the world view of the small child) to one that reflects the significance of belonging to a social group (comparable to Jung's task for young adulthood) to one that transcends the boundaries of groups (comparable to Jung's task for middle adulthood). Fowler does not assign chronological ages to his six stages, attesting to the reality that people progress at different rates. Many sisters' comments suggest, however, that they have moved from Fowler's Stage 3, Synthetic-Conventional, to Stages 4 or 5. (Fowler indicates that very few people, for example, Martin Luther King and Ghandi, ever reach Stage 6. This does not mean that sisters *cannot* reach that level, but that very few, indeed, do.)

Fowler defines Stage 3:

Stage 3 is a "conformist" stage in the sense that it is acutely tuned to the expectations and judgments of others, and as yet does not have a sure enough grasp on its own identity or faith in its own judgment to construct and maintain an independent perspective.[23]

He claims that Stage 3 individuals are found in both adolescent and adult populations; some make the transition out of Stage 3 in their late teens while others reflect Stage 3 thinking through both early and middle adulthood.

The Stage 3 person, very aware of her place in groups—religious, civic, social—manifests behaviors and attitudes consistent with the spoken and unspoken expectations of the group; she seeks the approbation of the institution as well as the authority representing it. Many midlife religious entered community directly from high school and wanted desperately to fit in and become model religious. Their efforts to keep the rule, to learn the office, and to develop appropriate manners are examples of this necessary growth stage in the developmental process; for these sisters, adherence to the externally imposed structures of prayer and living was absolutely essential for the maintenance of the community as well as their position within it.

Transition into Stage 4, Individuating-Reflexive, is characterized by decreased dependency on significant others as the individual critically assesses her own authenticity and the authenticity of the groups with which she is aligned. It is a step toward autonomy. "People at this stage hold themselves and others accountable for authenticity, congruence, and consistency in the relation between self and outlook."[24] Moving toward greater autonomy—a definition of self apart from the groups to which she belongs—can be a long and painful transition.

Frequently the transition from Stage 3 to Stage 4 is a somewhat protracted affair. The transition may begin around ages seventeen to eighteen, though we rarely find well-equilibrated Stage 4 characteristics before the early twenties. It is not uncommon to interview adults at all ages who are best described as 3-4 transitional types and who give evidence of having been there for a number of years. For some, the transition comes later, in the thirties or forties. When this occurs, it is experienced as a more profound disruption, often bringing a sense of temporary "breakup" as well as of "breakthrough."[25]

Sisters who previously found meaning and delight in the formal prayer expressions of the office, rosary, and community Mass (Stage 3) now want to assess those forms in relation to self-definition apart from community definition. The woman religious may seek alternate prayer styles—even alternate religions—to determine their authenticity for her. Although she still values her social group, she now realizes that this group, her community, possesses *a* truth, but not necessarily *the* truth. Personal prayer struggles during the Stage 4 transition are often compounded by interpersonal conflicts as the midlife wanderer is pressured by community members to attend common prayer and to participate in community religious services.

Transition into Stage 5, Paradoxical-Consolidative, is characterized by a synthesizing of the disparate discoveries of Stage 4. Fowler's description of the Stage 5 person is reminiscent of Jung's individuation process:

> When this process [Stage 5 thinking] becomes a natural part of an individual, "truth" comes to be a much more paradoxical reality than it was in Stage 4. Truth must be apprehended from a variety of standpoints. Stage 5 embraces and maintains the apparent contradictions or tensions that arise when truth is viewed from diverse perspectives. Though this often requires living with paradox, Stage 5 faith sees it as required by the character of truth.[26]

Transition from stage to stage is precipitated by tensions resulting from the inability to apply old solutions to new problems. The transitions involve more than finding something that will work; they involve an alteration of perspective—new thinking—which allows the individual to reconcile her emerging self-concept with her "grounding-in-being." Just as her self emerges throughout the life span, so also does her expression of that self—her prayer/faith life.

Some sisters find Fowler's system extremely helpful; they feel reassured knowing their questions, confusions, and dissatisfactions are, in fact, predictable stages in their faith development. Not all sisters share this enthusiasm. Finding his descriptions vague and academic, they prefer explanations that speak to their emotions rather than their intellect. These religious find greater solace in Sam Keen, a professor and student of faith development who relates the midlife transition directly to prayer dissolution.[27] A critic of Fowler's system, Keen speaks for many women religious when he notes:

> Jim Fowler's idealization of faith as a form of world coherence is a professorial typology of human development in which everybody ends up like a professor with a coherent view of the world. This notion of faith is largely masculine and is biased toward an intellectual way of being in the world. It makes little room for other types of persons, for what Jung referred to as sensation, intuitive, or feeling types.[28]

Keen sees the faith journey as a "letting go," an abandonment of control, rigidity, and certainty. The first half of life, he asserts, is a process of denying individuality and creativity by developing the control and "armor" required by social and religious sytems for acceptance—correct behaviors, correct prayer forms, correct communication styles. Midlife transition heralds a shattering of these defensive postures so that abandonment to trust—real faith—can emerge.

> Trust is manifested in a gradual or sudden yielding of the illusion of control and the concomitant loss of character and transformation of personality. What this means experientially is that the more I trust, the less I have to tie everything together. Trust allows me to tolerate plurality in the body and the body politic.[29]

Because so much of life is devoted to establishing and maintaining control, it is not surprising that religious who find their prayer lives falling apart in midlife scurry frantically to find someone or something that will help them "pull it back together"—get it under control. Many women religious enumerated difficulties they experienced when trying to pray during their midlife transition. Wanting desperately to find something that would "work," they experimented with prayer forms as if sampling food at a smorgasbord. Community prayer, office, prayer services, charismatic prayer, no prayer, shared prayer in small groups, and paraliturgical services were frequently attempted, entered into with great enthusiasm, and later abandoned as "not right" for them. It is in such abandonment of forms and formulas that the woman is faced with herself and her nakedness before her God. Realizing that there is little she can "do" to make prayer "work," she succumbs to her emptiness, admits to its pressure, and allows her god-within to speak. Keen asserts that this is when grace happens: "...in those moments when my controls are swept away or when I surrender and yield myself to a power beyond my control."[30] Trusting, surrendering to divine madness and creativity, is the faith task of the midlife wanderer.

Arriving at this resigned silence is no easy task. Midlife religious told many stories about struggling repeatedly with prayer before allowing silence, and most of them included anger, disappointment, frustration, and chagrin as companions of their struggles.

A common defense mechanism employed during various trouble points in the midlife transition is projection. Thus, it is not surprising that some blamed their prayer problems on the community, which "refused to try anything innovative"; others attacked the clergy and the institutional church for continuing "outdated, meaningless rituals that no longer speak." Some criticized God for failing them in their moment of need. "After all," said one, "I stuck with prayer when it was a real bore—when I had better things to do with my time. The least God could do is remember that now! Didn't all my efforts count for anything?" Until she abandons herself to trust, the midlife wanderer will seek both extrinsic (something "out there"—community, clergy) and intrinsic (something "in here"—prayer form, prayer style) sources of control; she pursues "ports in the storm" to which she can anchor her rootlessness. Although understandable, these behaviors are are ultimately futile; nothing short of contemplative trust, claims Keen, will suffice.

Keen is a developmentalist like Fowler, but he assigns different names to his stages. His stages afford a method for comparing sisters' reported development in prayer. The Child is passively dependent on others for approval and care; in the context of community, the sister who consistently looks to others to tell her how to pray and to reward her for her efforts is at the Child level of faith. The Rebel doubts, questions, and criticizes; the woman religious arrested at this stage in her faith development is negative, hostile, and even paranoid. Although some midlifers go through this stage—or maybe even get stuck in it—they are still very controlled and other-centered because of their strong reliance on extrinsics (persons, institutions) for their self-definition. To become adjusted, cooperative, and satisfied with the system is to enter into the Adult stage of faith development. Learning the rules of society, adapting to others, and compromising are necessary tasks of early adulthood; for Keen, they are insufficient for full development because they repress creativity through an exaggerated emphasis on control. An individual must move beyond the Adult and into the Outlaw stage for trust—faith—to happen. The Outlaw risks autonomy by standing outside of her system, by daring to descend into her soul, by challenging the control of the status quo within herself and within her community. To become an Outlaw is, for Keen, to enter into the midlife transition.

Outlaws are seldom understood and often ostracized, experiences familiar to midlife wanderers. To the observer the apparent fickleness of the midlife religious regarding prayer styles seems flighty, superficial, or careless; to the midlifer herself, the searching is an imperative. Even those who stop praying out of frustration report a sense of loss which more clearly than ever confirms their need for prayer, a need that perdures through whatever time their dark night encompasses. "Prayer shopping" in midlife is not a haphazard, frivolous seeking of an easy, accessible, and acceptable solution. On the contrary, it is conducted with great earnestness, and even desperation. Lay persons and religious alike report a need to turn to God differently during the turmoil of midlife transition; they *want* prayer—they *need* it, and will go to great lengths to find a prayer form that works for them. If this search demands that they become Outlaws, then they will suffer the consequences.

Just as few arrive at Fowler's final stage of faith, so also do few arrive at Keen's, the Lover and the Fool. Having tolerated the rootlessness of the Outlaw stage—viewing life from an autonomous perspective—the Lover and Fool possesses a cosmic appreciation of the interconnectedness of all life; she has distanced herself from her milieu to the extent that she now can embrace it as one expression of reality without ever ascribing to it the totality of reality. "The clue to the personality of the lover is that vulnerability and compassion have replaced defensiveness and paranoia. The lover has come back to the basic trust of the child. S/he is primarily *with*."[31] Keen's "with-ness" is the contemplation described by religious who have abandoned themselves to trust, to faith. It is also the integration of interiorization.

Whether sisters can relate to Fowler's explanation of faith development or Keen's, they learn that their prayer problems in midlife are predictable and necessary to total growth and emergence. Many do not have the benefit of "faith theories" against which to measure their growth; they learn from personal experience that everything, including prayer, falls apart and demands reintegration. Theories suggest generalities and provide directional markers along the path, but they cannot substitute for the uniquely personal task of living through the dark night of the soul.

A major difficulty described by many religious was their need to cope with the guilt of not being able to pray. Raised in the American work ethic mentality (Keen's "control"), they believed they could accomplish anything if they tried hard enough and worked long enough, and were convinced they had failed in discipline when prayer efforts were unfruitful. Their guilt was compounded by the anger they felt toward God for not rewarding their efforts and was exacerbated further for those who stopped praying altogether. To reestablish their spiritual integrity, these women had to learn that dry periods and dark nights were acceptable, growthful, and necessary stages in prayer, the seasons of the soul that deepen their appreciation of themselves and their relationship with their God. Although they had always known this intellectually, they did not understand it emotionally and spiritually; once a romantic ambience associated with the world of the mystic, the dark night of the soul is now experienced as it is—dry, dark, empty. A forty-nine-year-old sister described her experience:

> When I was a young sister, I envisioned the dark night of the soul to be like soft, black velvet. In my poetic imaginings, I looked forward to it, anticipating my plunge into the unknown which the mystics wrote about. Then I got there. It wasn't black velvet at all! It was scratchy sandpaper, ugly, and it hurt.

Some sisters questioned the impact of Vatican II on their midlife prayer problems, wondering whether their experiences would have been resolved sooner had they not had the latitude to experiment with such a variety of prayer forms. The answer is not available from the study's data, but comments from the study's participants suggest that the dark night of the soul is a unique phenomenon that occurs with unparalleled intensity in all prayer contexts. Trying to ascertain whether older sisters who had been restricted to few prayer forms had an easier time of it during their midlife transitions is, at best, unproductively speculative.

Midlife interiorization is a spiritual process, yet results indicate that women religious operating out of a primarily spiritual orientation are not thereby more primed for an easy transformation. It is plausible that religious, in fact, suffer a qualitatively different upheaval from lay persons precisely because it is their very foundation that is called into question.

Interiorization is a universal challenge of midlife, but it is experienced uniquely as each woman brings her personal history into introspective scrutiny. A spiritual journey, interiorization does not lend itself easily to discussion and analysis. Interiorization *is* the midlife transition, a shattering and rebuilding of the personality that emerges over time. Despite its elusiveness as a topic for discussion, interiorization can be studied in terms of its onset as well as its symptoms. For many, physical decline and awareness of death are the most commonly reported precipitating factors of the midlife transition.

---

1. C. G. Jung, ed., *Man and His Symbols* (New York: Dell, 1964). This text, which includes a chapter written by Jung, presents the basic tenets of Jungian psychology in a very lucid style and format. See also Joseph Campbell, ed., *The Portable Jung* (New York: Penguin Books, 1976).

2. Gerald O'Collins, *The Second Journey* (New York: Paulist Press, 1978).

3. Sheehy, *Passages.*

4. James Zullo, "The Crisis of Limits: Midlife Beginnings," *Human Development* 3, no. 1 (1982): 5-14, p. 7.

5. Levinson, *Seasons of a Man's Life,* especially chap. 4.

6. Vincent Bilotta, "Guilty: For Betraying Who I Am," in Kathleen Kelley, ed., *Guilt* (Whitinsville, Mass.: Affirmation Books, 1980), pp. 101-123, p. 108.

7. See Philomena Agudo, "Guilt: Its Effect on Wholeness," in Kelley, *Guilt*, pp. 17-32. All the articles in the Fifth Psychotheological Symposium are relevant to this discussion.
8. John Dunne, *The Way of All the Earth* (New York: Macmillan, 1972).
9. Clark Moustakas, *Loneliness* (Englewood Cliffs, N.J.: Prentice-Hall, 1961).
10. Dag Hammarskjöld, *Markings* (New York: Alfred A. Knopf, 1965), p. 85.
11. Loughlan Sofield and Rosine Hammett, "Experiencing Termination in Community," *Human Development* 2, no. 2 (1981): 24-31, p. 28.
12. Goldenberg, *Changing of the Gods,* especially pp. 54-64.
13. Ibid., p. 56.
14. Ibid., p. 61.
15. Margaret Mead, *Sex and Temperament in Three Primitive Societies* (New York: William Morrow, 1935).
16. See Hyde and Rosenberg, *Half the Human Experience,* especially chaps. 5 and 6. Another source exploring the effects of childrearing practices on sex-role behaviors is Caryl Rivers, Rosalind Barnett, and Grace Baruch's *How Women Grow, Learn, and Thrive* (New York: Ballantine Books, 1979). Both books contain excellent bibliographies for future reading.
17. Goldenberg, *Changing of the Gods,* p. 56.
18. Inge Broverman et al., "Sex Role Stereotypes and Clinical Judgments of Mental Health," *Journal of Consulting and Clinical Psychology* 34 (1970): 1-7.
19. Hyde and Rosenberg, *Half the Human Experience,* p. 119.
20. Goldenberg, *Changing of the Gods,* p. 59.
21. Hyde and Rosenberg, *Half the Human Experience,* pp. 62-69.
22. Jim Fowler, "Life/Faith Patterns: Structures of Trust and Loyalty," in Jerome Berryman, ed., *Life Maps* (Minneapolis, Minn.: Winston Press, 1978), pp. 14-101.
23. Ibid., p. 61.
24. Ibid., p. 70.
25. Ibid.
26. Ibid., p. 80.
27. Sam Keen, "Body/Faith: Trust, Dissolution and Grace," in Berryman, *Life Maps,* pp. 102-129.
28. Ibid., p. 103.
29. Ibid., p. 113.
30. Ibid., p. 112.
31. Ibid., p. 123.

Chapter 3

Midlife mourning: The wake of youth

The midlife woman struggling with interiorization is also in mourning, waking her youth, the first half of her life. Precipitated by a stark awareness of mortality, the transition is underscored by a realization of personal physical changes. A shift in the perception of time leads to preoccupation with health concerns and triggers an extended process of mourning her youth as a woman prepares to birth the second half of her life.

Approaching her late thirties and early forties, a woman faces death personally on several fronts. She confronts, first of all, the reality of aging or dying parents. She reverses roles, becoming a parent to her own parents, a shift that leads to a sense of loss and loneliness. Knowing that parents will die is one thing; seeing and accepting the fact is another. Though a fantasy, most adults act out a belief that parents will not die and abandon them.

On another front, the middle-aged individual witnesses serious illness and death in her friends. Often she says, "She's got cancer and she's so young—she's *my* age!" The midlifer must face the uncomfortable fact that, "If it can happen to other people my age, it can happen to me."

The third front on which mortality is met is the individual's own body. Even if she has kept in shape, the woman in her late thirties and early forties becomes increasingly aware of inevitable physical decline. She wears her first pair of bifocals, carries two bags of groceries instead of four, and is unable to run as long or as hard as her younger friends.

Summarizing the effects of physical changes on the midlifer's perception of self and time, Sean Sammon, F.M.S., notes:

> . . . in crossing the bridge between early adulthood and middle adulthood, men and women lose a sense of easy immortality, They begin to feel death in the marrow of their bones. There is, for example, no longer a generation standing as a buffer between them and death. Instead, middle-aged people become aware that they are now the dominant generation in society, looked to as a buffer against death by younger persons. The death of a contemporary is still eulogized as a tragedy but now serves as an acute reminder of one's own possible death through an accident or an illness. Even though an individual's physical changes may be measurably insignificant, at midlife graying or thinning hair is a grim reminder of age and ultimately of mortality.[1]

The combined effect of these events is a growing sense of helplessness which precipitates a numbing desperation and sometimes a paralysis.[2] Once the middle-ager accepts that death is inevitable and that time is limited, she rummages among the baggage of the past for signs of worth. "What have I really done with my life?" "What can I still do?" and "What does it really mean, anyway?" This questioning of values and personal meaning is the heart of the midlife turmoil. It is characterized by retreating into the self. To an observer, the midlife questioner appears withdrawn, preoccupied, and self-centered— which she is! Unfortunately, some mistake the preoccupation with death and physical change as the whole of the midlife transition, when it is actually only the focus of the early stages and a psychological impetus for challenging life goals and visions.

Physical changes in midlife

Articles on midlife accentuate the evident physical changes because proof of these is easily obtainable from physicians' records and insurance company reports; they are also easily observable in an American culture which idolizes youth. Women, more than men, are valued according to an imposed stereotype of picture-perfect beauty and slenderness carried to a point of physiological danger. The midlife woman has the dual task of overcoming social stereotypes about aging while struggling with personal acceptance of her unique physical changes.

Physical changes in the maturing person are inevitable, but the actual time at which they occur varies according to the individual's genetic code, diet, and exercise life-style.[3]

Height decreases gradually but measurably from age twenty-five on, the result of changes in muscle tissue, connective tissue, and bone density. The decrease is so gradual that most people are not aware of it until they are in late adulthood (sometimes after sixty years of age).

Strength, like height, increases to a maximum level through the mid-twenties, then declines steadily throughout the adult years. A 10 percent loss of strength occurs between thirty and sixty, affecting mostly the back and leg muscles. Great muscular effort becomes more difficult to sustain.

Reaction time peaks in the early twenties, then slowly declines. Adults compensate for both reduced strength and slower reactions through greater foresight and experience, a fact that accounts for fewer on-the-job accidents for older than for younger persons. In addition, adults learn to conserve strength for work over a longer period of time; they may not be able to keep up with younger adults in vigorous athletics that require bursts of energy, but are often able to outlast them in paced endurance. These gradual adjustments manifest themselves in changing recreational interests; adults trade their participation in quick-reaction sports like softball and tennis for walking, cross-country skiing and bicycling. Exercise and diet have a direct bearing on the extent to which an individual must adjust her activities, so adults who are sensitive to their needs for activity, exercise, proper rest, and diet can remain active and alert well into late and late-late adulthood.

Weight control is the major physical concern for adults. Metabolism slows down with aging, and this, combined with more sedentary activities, reduces caloric requirements. In spite of general knowledge about this basic physiological phenomenon, middle-aged people tend to eat as much as ever, and, as a result, begin to weigh more than ever. Moreover, the proportion of fat increases after age thirty even if weight remains the same. Weight gain is a problem in its own right, but it is even more insidious for the complications it induces, for example, stroke, heart attack, and hypertension.

Vision is constantly in flux; the eyes begin to age from birth onward, gradually changing shape. By fifty, most people require at least reading glasses because of farsightedness, a tendency that increases about tenfold between ten and sixty. Because the diameter of the pupil tends to decrease around fifty, brighter lighting is needed. The eyes lose their luster and sometimes begin to water more.

Hearing peaks around twenty, then gradually declines. The losses, often very subtle, tend to be more for high than for low tones. Today's music listening habits and urban noise pollution may accelerate hearing loss.

Taste sensitivity remains relatively constant until around fifty. At this age, persons can still distinguish sweet, sour, salty, and bitter, but may find it increasingly difficult to distinguish finer nuances of taste. Smell sensitivity decreases slightly after age forty, also affecting sensitivity to taste.

Sensitivity to touch increases until around age forty-five, then decreases sharply. Pain thresholds decrease after age fifty; hence, persons of this age tend to respond more vehemently to less pain.

Hair growth slows down with aging. Head hair for both men and women thins, according to genetic patterns, losing its luster. As hair loss is a side effect of birth control pills, more women today are balding. Hair growth in the nostrils and ears, and on the upper lip, chin, and breasts increases for aging women; these hairs tend to be thick and coarse.

As skin elasticity decreases with age and natural moisturizers dry up, more facial wrinkles and permanent "bags" appear under the eyes.

All these changes, which can sound rather dismal when cataloged, are predictable and generally slow to emerge; persons usually adapt to them as they occur, seldom noticing the changes at all. If educated to understand that all of these changes are normal, natural, and predictable, more adults might react to them less violently because, despite these rather awesome details, middle age is a time of peak physical health. Middle-aged adults suffer fewer acute illnesses but more chronic ones; persistent arthritis replaces frequent colds.

It may seem that the American emphasis on youth and appearance would have an adverse effect on the maturing adult's self-concept, but this is not the case. A 1973 study conducted by Ellen Berscheid, Elaine Walster, and George Bohrnstedt reveals that men and women over forty-five report just as much overall happiness with their bodies as those under that age. This satisfaction seems to result from gradual acclimation to subtle changes.[4]

Of those physical problems that do exist for the middle-aged group, the three most common are weight control, hypertension, and arthritis, respectively.[5]

Consistent with findings reported in the literature, 95 percent of women religious between the ages of thirty and sixty rated themselves in good-to-excellent health. Those who reported poor health—remarkably few of them—explained their situations as resulting from recent surgery or long-term disabilities like arthritis or diabetes.

Listing physical problems that concerned them, as many (26 percent of total reponses) cited tiredness as weight control as a major concern. Although there is a gradual reduction in stamina with aging, the awareness of it on the part of religious might be heightened by their very active lives, in which overwork and overextension are unfortunate occupational hazards. Weight control, the most frequently identified problem among the general public, is also a concern to religious. In addition to tiredness and weight gain, sisters listed arthritis, gray hair, wrinkles, impaired vision, high blood pressure, and thinning hair as changes they had observed in themselves over the years; few sisters found any of these to be serious problems, again substantiating the literature identifying the middle years as a time of peak physical condition.

Sisters value physical attractiveness; 97 percent rated it as important or very important. However, some qualified their responses by explaining that neatness and cleanliness were important whereas the fashion-plate look for its own sake was not. Some rated personal appearance as a low priority as a conscious reaction to the cultural pressure to conform to cover-girl looks and seasonal fashions.

> The importance of physical attractiveness has lessened since hitting thirty-seven, thirty-eight years.   [age forty]

I like to dress in simple but neat clothing.   [age thirty-three]

I seem to be more concerned now than I was before. I am very concerned about my hair, my face, the way I dress—and I seem to be more concerned now that I have come to know myself as a woman who is loved by men. I find I want to look attractive—at least I *admit* it now and I didn't before.   [age thirty-seven]

I had a difficult time coping with my obviously feminine body for a long time (36-26-35). I was, from about the 6th, 7th grade on, very breast conscious and felt overly uncomfortable about it. The habit mitigated my need to come to terms with this.... So, while I am realistic about "cover girl" looks, I *know* I am physically attractive. Being able to be "dressed up" is another factor here. I still feel "in costume" when dressed in current fashion or fully coordinated—in a self-conscious way.   [age forty-five]

I want to look clean, neat, groomed, but not [like] a fashion plate.
          [age forty-one]

My body is the framework, tool, instrument for my person and perception of reality. I try to keep myself whole by sensible diet, exercise and rest. I don't like interference by an inefficient machine.
          [age forty]

How I look makes a difference in how I feel.   [age fifty-two]

A pleasant personality—graciousness and cheerfulness—is more important than any physical beauty.   [age forty-eight]

Women religious, like adults in general, enjoy good health. They realize that physical changes are occurring, but are not overly concerned about them. They appreciate a neat, clean appearance and strive to maintain this through personal hygiene and wardrobe selection, but they are not driven to emulate Madison Avenue styles and fashions.

What about menopause?

Folklore has suggested that women experience midlife transition as part of menopause, an attitude consistent with the "anatomy is destiny" mentality which defines female personality in terms of hormonal balance. Existing midlife research, confirmed by women religious, reveals that menopause seldom has anything to do with midlife transition. The average age for menopause today is around fifty;[6] study results reveal that the midlife transition for the majority of women occurs in the late thirties to early forties—anywhere from five to fifteen years *before* the average age of menopause.

Although menopause is clearly not the midlife transition for women, material on the topic is included here for three reasons: (1) to address a basic physical phenomenon experienced by midlife women; (2) to present menopausal concerns and symptoms as reported by women religious; and (3) to shatter the myth that menopause is synonymous with a woman's midlife transition. Responding to the need for more empirical data on the topic, these results provide a description of the menopausal experience as it is reported by women religious, who do not fit the cultural stereotype of American women in general, that is, as coping with children, husbands, "empty nest syndrome," and sometimes limited educational backgrounds.

Menopause, like other physical changes, is a genetically determined event. Women whose mothers experienced a late menopause are likely to do the same. The average age for menopause today is around fifty, but it is normal for it to occur anywhere between the ages of thirty-five and sixty.

Menopause is the culmination of a process called the climacteric, the gradual decline in reproductive capacities over a ten-to-twenty-year period involving hormonal shifts similar to, but slower than, those in adolescence. Most women experiencing midlife transition are probably in the early stages of the climacteric, a fact borne out by the sisters participating in the study, only four percent of whom were under forty-five and menopausal. Sixty percent of the participants were premenopausal; 18 percent, menopausal; and 22 percent, postmenopausal.

Much is said about menopause, but surprisingly little has been really known about it until recently; more attention has been devoted to menarche. The more scarce the information, the more abundant the old wives' tales, frightening and confusing those who are approaching menopause unsure of what to expect. Traditionally, women have asked physicians about symptoms to be expected, and the physicians (who were, of course, educated about menopausal women by their own mothers, who were victims of unfounded fears and gossip about the event) sometimes perpetuated the myths. Unfounded statements about menopause include, "After menopause a woman is no longer a woman," "Menopause makes women crazy," and "Menopause marks the end of a woman's sexual desires and sexual attractiveness." David Reuben, referring to menopausal women in his book *Everything You Wanted to Know About Sex But Were Afraid to Ask*, did not improve the situation when he wrote, "Not really a man but no longer a functional woman, these individuals live in the world of intersex."[7]

Contemporary researchers are sorting fact from fancy. Investigating the concerns of both pre- and postmenopausal women, Bernice Neugarten discovered that younger women are likely to characterize menopause in terms of shared negative cultural fantasies, whereas middle-aged women consider menopause a far different experience.[8] Actually, only four middle-aged women out of one hundred reported fearing the experience; college-educated women were the least anxious of all participants about menopause. Neugarten and Ruth Kraines also learned that women in their teens and twenties were as likely as, if not *more* likely than, menopausal women to report crying spells, irritability, nervousness, depression, and excitability.[9]

Because women religious are quite well-educated, it is not surprising that they are generally well-informed regarding physical and emotional symptoms in menopause. That 28 percent are unsure of what to expect physically and 32 percent are unsure of what to expect emotionally supports the fact that too little solid information regarding menopause is yet available.

As to the sources of information for those premenopausal religious reporting knowledge of menopause, 38 percent learned from others' experiences, 31 percent from reading, and 15 percent from workshop attendance. Only 5 percent reported learning about menopause and its symptoms from physicians and these had had hysterectomies with some concomitant estrogen replacement therapy, suggesting that serious medical intervention heightens the possibility of a woman's turning to a physician for information about her experience.

The sources to which premenopausal religious would turn if they wanted information on menopause also reflects an educated stance: 41 percent indicated that they would rely on others' experience; 31 percent, on books; and 21 percent, on workshops on the topic. Only 3 percent indicated that they would go to physicians for information.

Reporting on their feelings about menopause, slightly more than 3 percent reported being very apprehensive; the majority, slightly more than 78 percent, indicated that they were not anxious at all. These results are consistent with Neugarten's findings that college-educated women in general are not concerned about menopause.

The responses of menopausal religious reflect an agreement with the responses of the subjects of other studies on a variety of related items.

The majority felt that they knew what to expect physically (66 percent) and emotionally (62 percent). Reading was the primary source of information (48 percent), and physicians were the second most popular source (17 percent). That more premenopausal than menopausal religious are relying on others' experiences might reflect a trend toward trust and appreciation of other women as a result of the feminist movement. It might also reflect a trend toward greater openness in discussing physical problems that were previously treated as private or even taboo.

There is no such thing as a "menopausal syndrome," a cluster of symptoms reported consistently by menopausal women. A study conducted in London during the 1970's revealed that only 10 percent of menopausal women suffered seriously and 10 to 50 percent did not suffer at all.[10] The most commonly reported symptom was hot flashes, but even these were not reported by all women. Comparable studies from other countries reveal similar results. Menopausal religious support these findings; of all symptoms listed, hot flashes were reported most frequently, and these were reported by only 30 percent of the women. No one symptom emerged as universal or even predominant, that is, with more than 50 percent frequency. Religious reported a variety of emotional symptoms, including hypersensitivity, moodiness, and depression, but did not reveal universal emotional symptoms nor even markedly frequent (more than 50 percent frequency) symptoms.

These and other studies' results suggest that physical and emotional symptoms associated with menopause might be culture-bound to the extent to which they are expected and reported. If symptoms are not well-documented, understood, and expected, the result is likely to be greater confusion and anxiety, culminating in a self-fulfilling prophecy.

In those cultures where women are increasingly respected in proportion with their age, women report few if any menopausal discomforts, especially depression. Pauline Bart, a sociologist, investigated the relationship between the "supermother" and menopausal depression, finding that women from cultures in which homemaking and childrearing were their primary responsibilities suffered more depressions than those from cultures in which they pursued careers and personal interests in addition to childrearing.[11] The "empty nest syndrome," which generally occurs around the late forties (close to the average age for the onset of menopause), is much more traumatic for "super moms" and consequently generates depression, an event that has been mistakenly attributed to hormonal shifts in menopause.

Addressing the correlation between hormonal balance and emotional stability, a popular medical treatment for the menopausal woman was at one time estrogen replacement therapy, a program aimed at controlling physical and emotional menopausal upsets. Drug companies, advertising their medications, urged physicians treating menopausal women to "put them on Premarin and keep them there."[12] Estrogen replacement therapy as the menopausal panacea was fortunately short-lived, for the dangers resulting from long-term hormone therapy became increasingly evident. Today's menopausal religious reflect the more conservative employment of estrogen replacement therapy; only 16 percent were on estrogen replacement and 12 percent on psychotropic (for example, Valium, Elavil, Librium) treatment. An overwhelming majority, 88 percent, were not worried about beginning menopause.

Reponses from postmenopausal religious provide an interesting comparison of age groups. The majority, 78 percent, were adequately informed about what to expect physically and emotionally. Sources of information were primarily others' experiences (29 percent) and their physicians (29 percent). Forty-eight percent reported hot flashes as the most frequently experienced physical symptom, again supporting the data indicating no overwhelming (more than 50 percent frequency) or universal symptom. Depression and crying were reported more frequently (35 percent) in the postmenopausal group than in the menopausal group (21 percent). More postmenopausal than menopausal religious had been treated with estrogen replacement therapy (50 percent) or psychotropic medication (31 percent). This increase might be explained by the fact that estrogen replacement therapy and psychotropic modalities were in greater vogue ten to twenty years ago than they are now.

An overwhelming majority, 94 percent, reported that they were not worried about beginning menopause, results consistent with Neugarten's findings for women in general. Reacting to their post-menopausal status, 40 percent indicted being "glad it's over," while others reported feeling more comfortable (30 percent) and emotionally steadier than before (25 percent). Such comments directly refute folklore claiming that menopause marks the end of a woman's life or that it drives her crazy.

Postmenopausal religious speak for themselves:

It's great! Those monthly inconveniences are over! I can live without fear of being embarrassed. Life seems to be freer. Although age is creeping too fast for me, I enjoy being over that hump in my life.
[age fifty-eight]

I simply made up my mind that I would go through it as calmly and naturally as possible. (I used a little mind control technique to keep me joyful and "on top.") I actually feel I can accomplish a lot more without the menstrual concern. I do feel a physical slow-down at times, but I attribute that to age/arthritis condition! Emotionally I feel greater fulfillment and sense of achievement!   [age fifty-one]

I think it's great! I know I'm getting older—but I feel good. I'm mentally alert—my body is not "playing tricks" with me. I take care of myself and physical changes are slower and expected. Brother Ass (St. Francis term) and I are comfortable together.   [age fifty]

I feel that we should live life to its fullest—not looking for things or feelings which "might" happen because of age.   [age forty-eight]

Inevitably, at least one woman religious participating in a midlife workshop asks, "Where does menopause fit into all this?" Her question reflects the culturally sustained myth that menopausal women—because of their menopause—are in midlife crisis. Until recently, there was little or no reliable information available to refute the myth, so women religious, like their lay sisters, were conditioned to believe that their midlife upsets were the result of hormonal imbalances. Inadequate information was compounded by unspoken conspiracies of silence which religious hesitated to violate. Bodily functions were not discussed during common recreation—*especially* bodily functions associated with the reproductive system! Fortunately, the situation is changing. As well-educated women, religious are learning the facts about their physical and psychological development. Armed with information and insights, they can assign menopause its rightful place in the developmental scheme, giving it attention proportional to its significance without succumbing to myths attributing to this natural bodily event magical powers over their physical and emotional well-being.

Midlife and time

Physical changes in adulthood, because of their inevitability, are a contributing component of the transitional turmoil. The changes come, uninvited. There is nothing the woman can do to will them away or to forestall their occurrence. She feels she is losing control. Even if a woman religious knows about and expects these changes, she often finds herself unable to cope with them within the context of the thought of death and illness which looms so ominously in her late thirties and early forties. A sense of time ebbing beyond her control frightens her; she feels helpless, drifting unanchored.

Time becomes a limited precious commodity.[13] Through this realization of limitation, the midlife wanderer is hurried into an audit of the time she has budgeted, banked, or invested so far and into an appraisal of what she can yet do with the dwindling account remaining.

Eighty-one percent of women religious responding to a question about changing time perceptions indicated that their conception of time had indeed changed; the average age of this realization occurred between thirty-five and forty, the period of midlife transition. Comments about the phenomenon reveal a variety of emphases.

Time began to change after the recent death of a few of my relatives. I now realize I am *mortal*.   [age forty-one]

It [time] goes faster than it used to.   [age forty-seven]

I feel a real "poverty" of time. I see so *much to do* and so little time to do it in. Time flies so quickly.   [age fifty-four]

More aware of and careful of the present moment.   [age fifty-six]

I am constantly surprised at *when* I am!   [age forty-eight]

[I see time] as precious. I really want to use it well, meaningfully. I find myself consciously choosing or planning to be with friends, rather than letting it happen by chance.   [age thirty-eight]

These comments support the literature predicting a sense of "time shift" during the midlife transition—a shift from viewing time as unlimited and extending into the future to perceiving it as very limited and existing right now in the present. Life is assessed in terms of years left to live rather than in number of years already lived.

Death awareness is closely related to the midlife realization of human "caughtness" in time. On one hand, there is still so much of the past that remains unfinished, so many unfulfilled plans and aspirations; on the other hand, the movement into the future continues to accelerate mercilessly. In adolescence I had little sense of limits; now I realize that my future is bounded by time and that much of it is already committed.[14]

Perceptions of a foreshortened future combined with illness and death in her family and among friends might thrust the midlife woman into an unprecedented obsession with her body and health. She may begin daily examinations, searching for the newest gray hair, the latest wrinkle, the possible lump, and the steadily upward swing of the bathroom scale.

Perhaps for the first time in her life she begins to read the obituaries.[15] Especially attuned to the ages of the deceased, she is upset to discover someone her own age; yet she secretly expects to find that very information, reinforcing the conviction that her own demise is imminent. Conversations center more and more on the details of hospitalizations, tragic deaths, and complicated medical procedures. Operations are discussed and scars exposed. The conversation of a group of midlifers might, for a time, become a medical "show and tell." If others do not take her fears seriously, a woman may become even more adamant in her insistence that she is, indeed, quite ill and deserving of attentions and sympathy. As in other areas of midlife concerns, however, some express these behaviors regularly, whereas others express few or none of them.

The midlife transition woman, despite the excellent health documented in midlife research, focuses so intensely on her body and its changes in an effort to cope with the inevitability of aging and eventual death. Upset when others, especially friends and physicians, do not take her seriously, she is frightened and confused as parents, friends, and younger people die around her, and is convinced that she will be next. Her health becomes an obsession as she reads every ache and pain as another indication that she is dying of some undiagnosed disease. Why not? Everyone else is dying; why shouldn't she? Her preoccupation with death precipitates the preoccupation with her own health.

Because midlife marks the inception of fewer acute illnesses but more chronic ones, it is very possible that the woman in her late thirties or early forties is developing one of these chronic diseases that require treatment. Attributing *all* complaints to hypochondriasis or "change of life" can be a narrow-minded, dangerous attitude. It is especially problematic for women, because research reveals that they are less likely to be taken seriously by their physicians than are men. As one physician writes, "The sexist attitudes of the medical community all too often interfere with adequate care for women,"[16] creating a systemic problem which further complicates the personal worries of the female midlife wanderer.

Whether healthy or ill, whether reconciled to limited time or not, the religious entering her midlife transition is directly confronted by the fact that she is no longer the young woman she used to be. Mirrors do not lie, parents do not recover from terminal illneses, and personal stamina is very evidently less reliable than before. Although the changes have been occurring all along, the woman seems to notice them for the first time. She is shocked, angry, dismayed, and confused. Actually, she mourns—she grieves the loss of her youth and her years. To deny the mourning is to deny life because mourning is the necessary psychological healing required after a significant loss in life. Just as physical surgery requires bodily recuperation, so does the psychological surgery of significant loss require spiritual healing.

The mourning process does not have a predictable time limit; it can last anywhere from a week to several years. Each person must deal with her unique loss in her unique way on her unique schedule.

Stages of the mourning process were first outlined by Elizabeth Kübler-Ross in her pioneering work *Death and Dying,*[17] and later expanded by Dorothy Heiderscheit, O.S.F.[18] After hearing them developed within the context of physical death and dying, Mary Jakubiak concluded that the stages were also applicable to the grieving of midlife, a conclusion endorsed by many midlife wanderers who heard the steps applied to them during midlife workshops. Some go through all the stages whereas others do not. Some experience the stages in the order discussed here whereas others do not. The structure of grieving is incidental to the grieving process itself. Understanding that certain reactions are typical and predictable helps the religious to feel affirmed while providing her with a vocabulary to describe her journey.

The first stage is shock and denial, epitomized in the statement, "This couldn't be happening to me." Reactions vary from the numb "business as usual" attitude to unbelieving protests of indignation. Some religious assert their denial by increasing demands on their schedules to prove to themselves and others that they can do just as much as ever. Others deny by resurrecting impossibly vigorous exercise programs that may have been daily fare in their teens but which are now dangerously taxing. Whatever the manifestations, the individual denies the obvious fact that she is getting older, that she is succumbing to the same aging process that overcomes everyone.

Denial is not necessarily pathological; it can be to the psyche what shock is to the body—a breathing space, a time to absorb the enormousness of a life-changing experience. Moral judgments about the evils of denial enter the picture only when the individual persists to the detriment of her own growth and adjustment. The person who flagrantly violates her physician's advice or who consistently exceeds the boundaries of common sense in good health care to prove that she is as young and fit as ever is flirting with health problems far more damaging than the aging process could ever be. Likewise, the woman who dresses in ridiculously inappropriate clothing to assert a youthfulness that is no more is ultimately harming herself by refusing to accept the greater self that she is—a gracefully maturing woman whose body is adjusting to the growth and aging process.

During the second stage of any grief work, emotions erupt. All that was pressing for expression following the first realization of shifting time and unwarranted change seems to explode at once. The midlife woman feels alone and lonely, believing that no one else understands the unique pain she is experiencing. She often voluntarily isolates herself to cry, rant, or curse, according to the bent of her personality, away from the mystified faces of the noncomprehending.

Hurt and anger characterize the third stage. Believing that life, community, and God have shortchanged her, she does not feel it fair for her to suffer so when she has led such a good, virtuous life. She begins to question the values of her life-style and her various mortifications, dedications, and ideals. "I don't deserve this. Why me? People living decadent lives deserve the signs of ravage—not me. It's not fair!"

The anger is violent and indiscriminate. It can be directed at any person or any thing as the midlife woman moving away from denial seeks an appropriate target for her wrath. She aggresses against herself because she is aging; she aggresses against the young because they *are* young; she aggresses against the old because they remind her of what she is becoming. Railing against God, the midlife woman demands a reasonable answer to what she perceives as her unreasonable plight. Working through this stage of grief is not pleasant to experience or to observe. The individual *knows* she is behaving irrationally but seems unable to do anything about it. She vacillates between unprompted outbursts and tearful apologies for them, only to repeat the cycle again and again. She feels trapped and protests her uninvited bondage by lashing out.

It is not uncommon for a woman to be unaware of the source of her anger during this stage, a situation ripe for employing the defense mechanism of projection. Blaming parents for refusing to change, for example, is one way projection might manifest itself in the grieving process. In fact, several midlife religious commented on their recurring frustration with their parents; "I want them to stop acting like old people! They're not old!" Underneath these criticisms is the paralyzing fear that she, the midlifer, will end up like them, the parents. Another manifestation of projection reported by many was criticism of and dissatisfaction with their communities' handling of the infirmary and retired sisters. Some protested the money spent to support the aged in communities while others questioned the trips, lectures, and special programs provided. Some simply refused to visit their sick and aging sisters because they "couldn't stand to be around them." Again, the infirmary itself is not the problem; the underlying issue is what it represents to the midlife religious who is angry about her own aging process.

Denial, emotionality, and anger are exhausting, so it is not surprising that during the fourth stage of mourning the midlife woman becomes ill. Her resources are depleted and her body is tired. She managed admirably for several months struggling through her early grief work, but she now succumbs to the toll taken on her body and psyche. Illness can result from physiological or psychological causes, but the result is the same—she feels sick. Illness allows a breathing space, a time to recoup energies and direction, providing the time and distance required for recovery and rearmament while imposing another distressing signal of imminent decline. What ensues is an approach-avoidance conflict; the individual wants and needs the resting time imposed by illness while she wants and needs not to be ill because of its statement about her reduced strength and resilience.

The outbursts of earlier mourning are replaced by panic and anxiety in the fifth stage. Overwhelmed by incontrovertible fact, the religious believes she is losing control—and losing her mind—as she frantically seeks answers and solutions, unable to concentrate, unable to sleep, unable to pray. Flitting from person to person and activity to activity, she questions, immediately dismisses answers, questions again. She may doctor-hop or house-hop, searching for some reliable person or activity to promise stability and reassurance. Not knowing what she can do now or in the immediate future further erodes her sense of rootedness. "What does this mean?" "What can I do about it?"

Friends and relatives, not always cognizant of the panic driving the midlife wanderer during this stage, often end up frustrated and angry at her refusal to follow their fine advice. "She asks for our help, then thinks nothing of ignoring it. How long can we put up with this?" Unfortunately, mutual frustrations can compound one another, destroying relationships and alienating people from one another. The distressed midlifer is not deliberately playing the role of the help-rejecting complainer, but is suffering the anguish of her personal inability to cope with changes occurring beyond her control.

Unable to find satisfactory solutions, the woman in the sixth stage of her grief work descends into guilt and self-blame. "I can't find the cause of this outside myself, so I must be the culprit." She reviews her life with a fine-toothed comb trying to identify the nits of transgression responsible for her current misery. This stage is characterized by the "If only..." syndrome: "If only I had exercised more...," "If only I had dieted better...," "If only I had prayed more...," "If only I had accepted that employment...," "If only I hadn't spent so much time at that one thing...." The list goes on, leaving no "if" unturned.

She tries to rectify what she believes to be unforgivable lapses in personal responsibility by imposing strict mortification regimes and by seeking forgiveness from those she perceives she has wronged. Guilt and blame become their own ends; the woman heaps both on her former self which she views as deserving nothing better.

The seventh stage evolves as depression and loneliness. Withdrawing from friends and activities, the midlife woman retreats to the solitude of her room and to the confines of her soul. She feels and acts sad; she is unable to respond to her friends' well-intentioned pleas that she "do something to snap out of it." Nothing seems worth the effort required. It is during this stage in the grieving process that the individual mourns both her past and her future somewhat as juxtaposed strangers passing over the threshold of her existence. She realizes that her energies, activities, enthusiasms, and friends will never exist again in the way she once knew and enjoyed them. Clinging to them, she now realizes, is futile, so she lets them go, painfully mourning their passing from her life. The midlifer tentatively embraces her future, aware that she is going into this uncharted territory a different person. She finally knows she will continue to be active and productive, but she knows also that her accomplishments will be somehow different because she is somehow different. Some hopes, dreams, and aspirations must be abandoned; youthful visions must be modified. Ceasing to wonder what she has done with all her years so far, the midlife woman begins to accept that it is humanly impossible for her to accomplish all that she had hoped for in her late teens and early twenties. Her mental meanderings are bittersweet as she recognizes that many of her ambitions were fantasy, an insight that rocks her conception of herself as rational and competent. Changing the Church, challenging the community, developing a superself were all noble aspirations which remain elusively distant, forcing the midlifer to acknowledge that her expectations exceeded the human limitation of aging. Cherished goals must be revised and made more reasonable. Thus, the depression of this grieving stage is both reactive and anticipatory, requiring time, solitude, and understanding. It is the descent into essential loneliness.

Reentry troubles accompany the eighth stage of mourning. Having arrived at some sense of peace about herself, her past, and her future, the woman is now ready to begin living the new life she has fashioned for herself but is unsure of how to proceed because of changes that have occurred during her emotional and physical absence. Like a traveller returning from a long journey, she looks around with caution and wonder, amazed that so much of the external looks the same, yet frightened because so much of the internal has changed. She remembers her irrational outbursts of earlier phases and is uncertain how others will respond to her now. She recalls her withdrawal and silence and worries that others will keep her at arm's length, assuming that she wants more of the same. "Will they forgive me?" she asks; "Will they accept me?" If her mourning has been protracted, the midlife woman may be faced with the very real difficulty of catching up on considerable amounts of work; this task in itself can be overwhelming. Attempting to reestablish a "business as usual" routine in relationships and work results in yo-yo feelings—one minute she is resolute and determined, the next minute frightened and insecure.

Finding that she can, in fact, return to life with dignity and determination, the midlife religious enters the ninth stage of grief work, which is characterized by hope, Seeing the light at the end of the tunnel, she wants to get out and on with life and work. Having come to grips with her body, her age, and her future life goals, she is eager to apply her new insight and enthusiasms to daily living. All is not resolved; the ninth stage of grieving is an up-again, down-again experience as the practical working out of her reentry evolves. Taking her daily successes as proof that she can and will survive, she finds that the good days begin to outnumber the bad. Hope increases as peace and success return.

The tenth and final stage of grieving is the affirmation stage wherein the midlife religious understands, accepts, and embraces the person she is. No longer young, but not yet old, she is filled with a new kind of strength and life as she undertakes the second half of her life journey. Pangs of youthful longings recur, but she is now comfortable with them and makes no mistakes about identifying exactly what they are as she incorporates them into midlife wisdom. Because her energies are no longer tied up with fighting the inevitable, she can employ her strength to resolve the midlife philosophical questions, which, according to Jung, are the crux of the midlife transition. The mourning of youth must occur before midlife can begin; it is the resurrectional prerequisite for midlife introspection and interiorization.

Not every midlifer goes through every stage of grief, nor does she go through them in the order presented. Some stages are short, others long; some are suffered consciously, some unconsciously. Personal style affects expression. The danger inherent in a discussion such as this is that the midlifer may be tempted to treat an explanatory outline as a checklist against which she can measure herself—or diagnose others!

Religious hearing these steps applied to midlife responded with relief. "That's exactly what I was trying to tell you," commented one sister to another during a midlife workshop reviewing these stages.

"It's saying what I said. You didn't seem to understand me then; *now* does it make sense?"

Many expressed enthusiasm, reassured by the outline. "Not only can I better understand my confusing reactions," said one, "but I now have the vocabulary to express them."

Midlife mourning is a new and unique experience for the midlifer, so it defies comparison with earlier life events and often leaves a woman rudderless to herself and an enigma to her friends. Midlife workshop participants expressed appreciation for this explication of the grieving process applied to their unique maturing through midlife transition.

The mourning process has a specific precipitating cause—awareness of aging and mortality. Although it often precedes the work of interiorization, it can also occur simultaneously with it. Numerous symptoms manifest themselves throughout both processes—anger, rebellion, prayer problems, sexuality crises, and career changes—all of which are *part* of the transition or *results* of the transition, but none of which *is* the transition. Understanding interiorization and mourning as the substance of this developmental process, we will now turn our attention to the various expressions of the turmoil—the symptoms themselves.

---

1. Sean Sammon, "Life after Youth: The Midlife Transition and Its Aftermath," *Human Development* 3, no. 1 (1982): 15-25, pp. 20-21.

2. Levinson, *Seasons of a Man's Life.* See also Elliott Jaques, "Death and the Mid-life Crisis," *International Journal of Psychoanalysis* 46, no. 4 (1965): 502-514, and Bernice Neugarten, "The Awareness of Middle Age," in Bernice Neugarten, ed., *Middle Age and Aging* (Chicago: University of Chicago Press, 1968).

3. Lillian Troll, *Early and Middle Adulthood* (Monterey: Brooks/Cole Publishing, 1975). Troll's outline of physical changes in midlife is presented in the following pages.

4. Ellen Berscheid, Elaine Walster, and George Bohrnstedt, "Body Image," *Psychology Today* 7 (November 1973): 119-131.

5. Edwin Bierman and William Hazzard, "Adulthood, Especially in the Middle Years," in D. W. Smith and E. Bierman, eds., *The Biologic Ages of Man* (Philadelphia: Saunders, 1973), pp. 154-170.

6. Janet Hyde, *Understanding Human Sexuality* (New York: McGraw-Hill, 1979), especially chap. 4.
7. David Reuben, *Everything You Always Wanted to Know About Sex* (New York: David McKay Company, 1970), p. 292.
8. Neugarten, *Middle Age and Aging.*
9. Bernice Neugarten and Ruth Kraines, " 'Menopausal Symptoms' in Women of Various Ages," *Psychosomatic Medicine* 27 (1965): 266.
10. Sonja McKinlay and Margot Jeffreys, "The Menopausal Syndrome," *British Journal of Preventative and Social Medicine* 28 (1974): 108. See also Hyde, *Understanding Human Sexuality.*
11. Pauline Bart, "Depression in Middle-aged Women," in V. G. Gornick and B. K. Moran, eds., *Women in Sexist Society* (New York: Basic Books, 1971).
12. Estelle Fuchs, *The Second Season* (New York: Anchor Press/ Doubleday, 1977).
13. Rogers, *The Adult Years,* and Kimmel, *Adulthood and Aging.*
14. Zullo, "The Crisis of Limits," p. 11.
15. Fried, *Middle-Age Crisis.*
16. Penny Budoff, *No More Menstrual Cramps and Other Good News* (New York: Penguin Books, 1980), p. 295. This is a very well written, informative book on women's health care written by a woman physician.
17. Elizabeth Kübler-Ross, *Death and Dying* (New York: Macmillan, 1969).
18. Dorothy Heiderscheit, O.S.F., is a therapist at Counseling Services for Religious and Clergy in Dubuque, Iowa. She outlined the ten stages of grief as part of a "Stress and Grief" workshop conducted during Spring 1981 for the Sisters of St. Joseph of Cleveland, Ohio.

Chapter 4

Assuming adult status:
The generation gap

Midlife mourning and individuation, highly personal, unique events, do not lend themselves readily to academic dissection; although they constitute the heart of the transition, they often go unrecognized as such because of their highly individualized expression. As total experiences, however, they affect all aspects of the midlifer's existence, generating symptoms of upheaval and dissatisfaction which manifest themselves as family conflicts, altered perceptions of community and civic authority, career discord, and vocational crises, all of which are quite visible and more accessible to study and documentation. Symptoms of the midlife transition tend to occupy center stage as *the* midlife transition precisely because of their availability to scrutiny. They are authentic phenomena deserving serious attention but must never be understood, either singularly or together, as the totality of the experience.

Family relationships

As she enters her late thirties and early forties, the woman in transition becomes part of the 20 percent of the population referred to as the command generation, that segment of society responsible for administering religious communities, establishing and enforcing policies, and controlling institutions. She is in an enviable yet awesome position. She acquires success and status commensurate with her experience and age, enjoying the actualization of many cherished ideals as she applies her talents and gifts to her work; yet she realizes the tenuousness of it all as she experiences pressure and threat from the older generation, reluctant to relinquish *its* power and influence, and from the younger generation, eager to assume *its* place of command and influence.[1] The midlifer in command is torn between maintaining the status quo and moving boldly ahead to where her visions and ideals direct her. Trapped in a double-bind, she struggles with self, family, community, church, and society to define her emerging place within the private and cosmic order. Her search for definition and stability brings her into conflict, both intrapersonally and interpersonally, with people and systems closest to her, a situation that effects vacillation between resentful passivity and truculent aggression.

Family relationships are generally felt most poignantly. The midlifer who competently executes her professional responsibilities, successfully adapts to changing community structures, administrates institutions, and writes policies that affect the Church and the world is chagrined to realize that she still is—and fears she always will be—her parents' little girl. She senses her parents' pride in her accomplishments but is nevertheless resentful of their posture of protection and control.[2]

The conflict between midlifers and their parents is mutually painful. Parents, who have functioned for years as mentors, counselors, providers, and protectors, are reluctant to relinquish their roles; even if they are being cared for by their adult children, they know from personal life experiences that there is a "better way" to make decisions, manage money, or cook a meal, and they do not hesitate to say so. Their input has been valued and appreciated until now; why shouldn't it continue to be? Indignant and hurt, they desire to remain involved in their children's lives out of interest and concern but are increasingly reluctant to do so as they encounter rejection and resistance. Personal fears of aging exacerbate parents' unwillingness to relinquish control as they cope with what they perceive to be their children's lack of appreciation for past sacrifices, current interest and advice, and wisdom.

The midlife woman, for her part, is caught in a role conflict as she attempts to alter her status from the child-daughter to the adult-daughter. She wants to appreciate and enjoy her parents and, at the same time, to be respected by them for her competence and maturity; she wants to discuss her accomplishments and dreams with them, but is tired of their editorial comments on her activities and methods. Just as parents expect appreciation from their children for all they have given them over the years, so too does the midlife woman expect appreciation from her parents for all she is doing for them now, especially if they are elderly or ill and require her time and energy. The tug-of-war between daughter and parents for respect and influence is highly emotional and consequently painful because of the unarticulated expectations that surround the conflict. As one forty-six-year-old sister complained in exasperation after returning from a visit to her semi-invalid father, "Why do I keep going [over there]? I clean, cook, play cards, listen to his problems—and all I hear about is how I'm doing everything wrong. God help me if I mention politics! He's so much as told me I don't know what I'm talking about."

The midlifer's feelings toward her parents are often ambivalent—she loves and appreciates them but at the same time she resents their control. She knows they are aging and will not be around forever, a fact that angers and saddens her because it presages the future that awaits her. Past memories loiter to be enjoyed; past hurts cry to be healed. The "shoulds" and "oughts" of childhood years, outgrown by the maturing person, wait to be dismissed and replaced by a more realistic understanding and acceptance of human growth and limitations as responsibilities shift from parents to their children.

Declaring adult status within the family constellation is a different experience for men than for women. For Levinson's men, assumption of adult status within the family is just one among many ways in which the middle-aged man asserts his maturity and independence; his growth and competence, which have been encouraged from youth onward, are finally manifested in *all* facets of his life, including his primary family.[3] For women who have seldom or never been encouraged to develop competence and independence, the assumption of adult status demands that they first develop autonomy, then express and effect it.

Social conditioning plays an enormous role in men's and women's development, and scientists are now identifying how this occurs. Through differential child-rearing practices, parents subtly and overtly teach young boys to be independent, achievement-oriented, and competent, whereas they teach young girls to be passive, dependent, and incompetent.[4] For example, boys' bedroom decor, often characterized by visually stimulating wallpaper, pictures, and mobiles, encourages exploration and discovery; their rooms are filled with action-oriented toys (trucks, erector sets, puzzles) and their furniture is selected to withstand typical child use, that is, colors are dark, dressers and desks are sturdy, and work spaces are plastic-coated. Girls' bedrooms, by constrast, tend to be visually bland and nonconducive to active play and exploration. Gentle pastels, fluffy rugs (which get dirty quickly), and frilly ruffles and dresser scarves mitigate against girls' active involvement in their environments. Quiet play with a few dolls or playhouse is about all these rooms can physically take! In their actual play, boys who are unable to pound a peg into a board successfully are encouraged to try it again until they "get it right" whereas girls confronted with the same dilemma are generally helped to complete the task. Boys' games, generally played in large groups, demand physical skills while developing a sense of competition and survival; girls' games require quiet involvement on a one-to-one or small-group basis, eliciting cooperation and docility.[5] Because they are expected to compete in the "cold, cruel world," boys are encouraged to stand on their own and fight for their rights—no one is going to take care of them if they cannot care for themselves. Both parents convey this message to their sons because they expect them to move from home base to seek fame and fortune in the competitive marketplace. The adage "A son is a son 'til he takes a wife; a daughter's a daughter the rest of your life" summarizes the social expectation that sons are on loan—daughters are permanent parental property.

While the son is learning that he is ultimately responsible for himself and his survival, the daughter is learning that "someone else" will take care of her. She is more often rewarded for being passive, cooperative, and sweet than for hitting the winning home run or defending herself against neighborhood bullies. To be too competent, too successful, or too competitive is discouraged in little girls; they are told that it is unladylike to behave this way and that no one will like them if they persist in their "tomboy" behaviors. The key message to the developing girl is clear: it is more important to be likable than it is to be competent.

If her parents are atypical, or if she fails to absorb the "dependency message" of childhood, by adolescence the girl is reminded by her high-school social group—now *the* focal point of her self-identity— that she is more acceptable when demonstrating so-called feminine behaviors than she is when exhibiting competency behaviors. Hyde and Rosenberg call this female adolescent crisis the "achievement-femininity incompatibility conflict."[6] Society's dictate to the developing child is achievement; to get good grades, to develop physical competencies, and to learn social skills are the tasks of elementary-school children of both sexes. Girls are generally encouraged in these skills, especially academic ones, as much as boys are. But in high school, the picture changes for girls. They are now told that they must be feminine; to be feminine is to be passive, dependent, popular, acceptable—qualities antithetical to developing competence and independence. If she persists in her childhood achievement ambitions, pursuing good grades and struggling to compete for academic and athletic honors, the adolescent girl finds herself shunned by males and females alike for her "unladylike" behaviors. To attain social acceptance, she learns that she must become less success-oriented and more other-oriented, that is, make and remake her personality to meet societal expectations of popularity, acceptability, and cooperation. Hyde and Rosenburg summarize the dilemma:

> If the girl continues to achieve she will be unfeminine, and to be feminine is not to achieve. The girl is caught in a situation in which two equally important systems of values are in conflict. One is the desire for a positive sense of self, the sense that one is a worthwhile, productive person. Achieving, getting good grades, and excelling have been encouraged and rewarded so far, providing a major avenue for establishing the self as having worth and value. But the reward system changes abruptly at adolescence. The competing system is the desire to

be a good female, to conform to gender-role expectations, and to be feminine, with whatever rewards that carries.[7]

Parents, who have been as indoctrinated with these expectations as their daughters, unwittingly reinforce social pressures for femininity by expressing greater delight over their daughter's invitation to the prom than over her straight-A report card. Her social success becomes their parental success; conversely, her social failure becomes theirs. Popular stereotypes of the "poor parents" saddled with an unmarried (read: unacceptable) daughter heighten the pressure placed on parents to encourage their daughters in the prevailing passivity pattern for females established and rewarded by society.

To be feminine is to be mentally unhealthy and personally unfulfilled. Mothers, who have devoted their lives to caring for and pleasing others (that is, to living out society's prescribed feminine role), find themselves in conflict regarding their daughter's upbringing. If the mother encourages her daughter to follow the traditional path for a female, she knows she is dooming her offspring to a potentially deadening and deadly future; if she encourages her to risk violation of social stereotypes by becoming competent and successful, she is exposing her daughter to potential rejection—and possibilities for success that far exceed her own. Maternal ambivalence, which operates unconsciously, is masked in "smother love," that is, an emotional symbiosis in which neither mother nor daughter can live without the other although both desire autonomy and self-expression. Nancy Friday, critiquing mother-daughter relationships in her book *My Mother, Myself*, articulates the unique problems surrounding this explosive relationship;[8] Madonna Kolbenschlag amplifies the message in *Kiss Sleeping Beauty Good-Bye*.[9] Both authors note the love-hate, trust-mistrust tensions permeating mother-daughter interactions; they identify the symbiotic ties between mothers and daughters encouraged by a society that sanctions less-than-mature development for women, thus creating an environment in which women alternately cling to and compete with one another—rather than cooperate with one another—for identity and self-esteem. None of this is to suggest that mothers deliberately conspire to thwart their daughters' growth! Naming the problem is not intended to perpetuate the insidiousness of blaming the victim but rather is directed toward greater understanding of the problem. Summarizing the situation, Janet Ruffing, S.M., writes, "[Nancy] Friday contends that most women are still concerned with unfinished business related to mother-daughter relationships. She asserts that our emergence into a fully autonomous identity requires the working through of unresolved ambivalences in this primary relationship."[10]

Levinson contends that a major task of midlife transition for a man is the establishment of an adult identity with his parents. The male's identity formation, begun in childhood and formulated in adolescence and young adulthood, is simply crystallized as he enters the second half of his life. The woman's transition is neither as linear nor as logical! Parental and societal expectations have actively encouraged her *not* to develop a unique identity; they have told her that others will take care of her, that she need not take care of herself. Whereas the midlife male is effecting a continuation of the identity process begun in childhood, the midlife female is *beginning*, for the first time in her life, to formulate a personal identity apart from childhood and adult dependencies. Through her individuation work, the midlife religious confronts herself as a *self*, emerging with a declaration of independence as new to her as to those around her. A thirty-seven-year-old described her journey through this painful land:

> My dad died when I was twenty-three and at thirty I began to work through his death—having reached a point of being able to admit that I was angry that he wasn't more responsive and didn't show his love and affection by words or touch. Mother is living and is the dominant person in my life. I'm only now realizing how angry I am that she has taught me to be the "good girl" at all times. Only now am I beginning to be "myself" when I am with her—no longer the "little girl."

Another sister could have been thinking about Friday's book when she wrote:

> [I have] a growing awareness of characteristics which I have that are the same as my mother's—and not wanting to strengthen some of those. [I'm dealing with] my tendency to feel anxious that I don't visit home more often plus a sense of guilt that mom would like it otherwise.   [age forty]

Although all midlifers experience conflict with their parents, the problems are accentuated for women and especially for women religious who have straddled pre-and post-Vatican II conventual styles. Prior to the Council, women entered community directly from high school; they were very young and still quite dependent upon their parents for emotional, social, and sometimes financial support. Some parents resisted their daughter's vocational decision, but the majority accepted it, coming to the convent for monthly visits, driving their daughter to and from doctor's appointments and summer school, and, when possible, providing small gifts and pocket cash for their "daughter who had given up so much." Unfortunately, such practices generated family interaction patterns that extended filial dependency for the religious well into her twenties and thirties—sometimes even beyond that. Post-Vatican II alterations in religious life-style initially compounded the dependency for many, because they became free to make home visitations—which were often gala events—and to accept gifts of clothing and cash to facilitate the transition from traditional to secular garb. Again, the beneficence of parents made much of this possible, and their religious daughters were often, even if somewhat reluctantly, willing to accept the largess.

As the changes accelerated, women religious became increasingly independent of their parents as well as of their traditional "parenting" community structures. Evolving new theologies, experimenting with new prayer forms and new community living situations, these women would return to visit with parents who often neither understood nor accepted many of the changes in the Church, let alone in their daughters! Perhaps for the first time in their religious careers, sisters were meeting opposition and even rejection from the very parents who, ten years earlier, could not do enough for their "daughter, the nun." Necessary attitudinal growth was slow and culminated for many in a new family stance during the midlife transition.

Ninety-two percent of women religious polled acknowledged a change in attitude toward their parents, and the most frequently reported age at which the attitudinal change was noticed was between thirty-five and forty. This suggests that assumption of adult status within the family is a midlife issue for women as well as for men, even if the process of resolution is qualitatively different for the two sexes.

Comments about their attitudes toward parents reflect appreciation, anger, and a need for adult relationships within the family. Some have intensified their love for and gentleness toward their parents while others have arrived at peace only after working through histories of hurt and misunderstanding.

> Parents are more my friends now. We spend time together because we enjoy one another. Communication is freer, deeper. [age thirty-nine]

> At around twenty-eight I was angry at my parents for raising me as they did. At age thirty-eight I was able forgive them, knowing they raised me in the only way they knew how to.   [age forty]

> While a member of the Novitiate, I remained a child to my parents; it was comfortable. Then, one day, we had a significant talk and I became "adult with adult." Now, my parents are elderly and child-like. In many ways I've become parent to them.   [age forty]

> I tried to be a friend to my mother but she could not go past the parent/child syndrome. I believe she resented my adult independence and assertiveness as a woman religious especially after renewal in community.   [age forty]

Results from this and other research indicate that the establishment of adult status with parents is a midlife transition task. However, results also suggest that women religious are assessing their independence/dependence in relation to their parents prior to midlife. This is probably the result of more information on the topic in addition to an increased awareness of personal and adult identity issues among women religious and women in general. Although the majority of women religious indicated the thirty-five-to-forty age bracket as the time when they first noticed a change in their feelings toward their parents, a substantial number, 44 percent, indicated some attitudinal changes toward their parents *before* the age of thirty-five. It seems that establishing adult-to-adult relationships with parents is a process emerging over time; recognizing parent-child dependencies in her early thirties allows the woman religious to assess and prepare for the actualization of this task in midlife transition. Being aware of changes and dealing with them are two different matters. It is possible, through altered childrearing practices and development of greater autonomy in adolescent females, that women of the future will become adults to their parents sooner in their life span. Current results suggest that children struggle to become adults to their parents as a midlife task; how long this will be the case remains to be seen.

Whatever the future, contemporary religious report an evolving awareness of self as an adult reponsible for decisions and their consequences. Realizing that they could not forever remain their parents' daughters, religious struggled to attain adult status with their parents while assuming greater caretaking responsibilities for them. Some were able to come to terms with themselves and their parents through discussions and confrontations; others resolved their conflicts within themselves after a parent's death. Not wanting to be disrespectful, but not wanting to be dependent either, the midlife wanderers reported attaining adult status with their parents as one of the most difficult transition tasks.

In addition to striving for adult status with parents, some women religious struggle to attain adult status with their brothers and sisters as part of their midlife developmental transition; others—the majority—resolve sibling relationships prior to midlife. Siblings are in a somewhat similar situation, after all, for they share the common problem of establishing an identity apart from the parents. A forty-six-year-old religious noted that the death of her parents united her more closely than before with her brothers, while a thirty-six-year-old wrote, "I relate more affectionately to them and allow them to relate more affectionately to me."

Although most religious were quite positive about their relationships with siblings, all were not. Some complained about family conversations that focused on children and jobs while excluding them and their interests. Others minded the "snide" comments slipped in regularly at family gatherings about "the good sister" who "has it so easy."

A forty-six-year-old religious returned from a week-long family reunion (the first in her family in over twenty years) with very mixed feelings and reported a scenario common to the dramas retold by many others in this area of sibling tensions.

> I enjoyed seeing them again, being with them. But I'm glad we don't do that very often. My sister jumped all over my brother (a religious priest) and me, accusing us of living Pollyanna lives devoid of financial worries. She claimed that we didn't know what life was all about. I don't know why I argued with her; my brother kept saying, "Let it go—she doesn't understand. Just let it go." I guess I mind that I'm expected to learn all about her life and her concerns but that she doesn't make any effort to understand mine.

Another sister, forty-four years old, almost came to blows with her brothers and sisters following placement of their father in a nursing home. She felt that they should assume a greater proportion of the visiting because "they had nothing to do in the evenings" whereas she was busy with class preparations and community responsibilities. They disagreed, pointing out that they were paying the bills; they felt she could assume her share of the responsibilities by spending more time with the father since she did not have the burden of children and home duties. They all suffered in their mutual recriminations until they were able to progress beyond complaining to working out an acceptable schedule of visiting and caretaking.

Since all men and women must eventually seek adult status with their parents, it is not uncommon for grown siblings to support one another through their unique parent-child struggles, thus drawing brothers and sisters into adult friendshps with one another. Women religious are no exception. The advent of greater freedom for interactions with family may have heightened familial conflicts for contemporary midlife religious, but it may also serve to facilitate resolution of these for future generations. In the meantime, adults will continue growing toward mature identity and will encourage their parents to recognize the growth; parents may resist, but their adult children will persist. They must become their own adults to live the second half of their lives—as they fashion it—without parental permission.

Authority in community

Developmental psychologists identify a power shift that occurs during midlife transition when the emerging midlife wanderer is expected to assume greater responsibility at work and in the community. To effect this shift, midlifers must revise many of their former notions about authority and its legitimacy, abandoning absolute confidence in authority and power structures while reconciling the arbitrary nature of power and those who hold it with their own newly assumed power. Resolution of these conflicts is the primary task of the destruction/creation polarity discussed earlier, but philosophical conclusions take physical form in the power shift of midlife.

Levinson found that the men in his study struggled with power issues as part of their midlife transitions;[11] they were promoted to social roles invested with considerable prestige and were expected to execute their responsibilities for the "promotion of the institution and society." Desiring to succeed in these positions, many men wrestled with tensions between effecting radical change and maintaining the status quo to minimize upset. Some discovered their freedom hampered by older, newly displaced authority figures insisting on being heard—after all, they had controlled things for twenty years or more—and their spontaneity threatened by younger, ambitious men seeking their place on the hierarchical ladder. Resolution of these tensions, including alterations of attitudes toward authority, was problematic for many.

To what extent do women, typically denied positions of authority and socially conditioned to depend upon authority, wrestle with authority issues in midlife? Furthermore, to what extent would women religious, who often moved from mother at home to mother superior in the convent, resolve authority conflicts within themselves and their communities? Is any of this even a midlife issue for women and women religious?

A striking majority of women religious, 96 percent, indicated a change in their attitudes toward authority in the convent. That attitude shift is primarily a midlife issue is reflected in the fact that the most frequently reported age for change was between thirty-five and forty, but that attitude change is not *exclusively* midlife material is evident in the 46 percent who reported attitude change prior to age thirty-five. Whatever their feelings toward authority when they entered the convent, 85 percent had changed their perceptions of it by the time they were forty years old.

Altered perception of authority, though a documented midlife phenomenon, is not explained exclusively in midlife terms for religious.[12] Although there is an obvious correlation between the midlife transition and attitude change, the explanation also includes recent developments in social attitudes, in psychological awareness, and in community structures that emerged following Vatican II. Terms like "collegiality," "collaborative leadership," "enabling leadership," and "corporate direction" are familiar vocabulary in religious life since the late 1960s.[13] Realizing that archaic, outmoded hierarchical organizations of community leadership were detrimental to maturity in religious life, community women investigated alternative styles of leadership and experimented with them through their lived experience in both small and large group settings. Alterations in community leadership structure encouraged women religious to think through authority issues prior to their midlife transitions. One thirty-nine-year-old sister commented:

> I never really bought "blind obedience" but was probably pretty close to it. However, in the Juniorate when personal spiritual needs were being denied, I began to read more and discuss more regarding personal responsibility—no longer believed or wanted my "superior" to be responsible for my actions—positive or negative.

Attributing all changing perceptions of community authority to Vatican II mandates is as overly simplistic as ascribing all changing perceptions to midlife reassessment. Social challenges, including those stemming from Third Force psychology, affected perceptions.[14] Authority—particularly institutional authority—was questioned and reevaluated by persons committed to controlling their own destiny. That much of this questioning was valuable is evident in the more deliberate, critical stance of the individual religious assessing the validity of "absolute proclamations" for her personal integration. Seeking greater self-understanding, and willing to assume responsibility for that search, many religious wrestled with personal/

community authority questions throughout their twenties and thirties and beyond. Acceptance of personal responsibility often generated greater sensitivity to authority figures—a shift evident in the remark of a forty-one-year-old religious: "Those in authority are human with the same needs, strengths, limitations as everybody else. I try to relate to them that way."

From a developmental perspective, the woman religious who entered community directly from high school matured from child to adolescent to adult status within community, a progression affected by many social and ecclesiastical changes throughout the past twenty years. In her late teens, the contemporary religious left her parenting family, where often she had been conditioned to dependency and passivity, to align with a religious organization whose leadership structure paralleled established authority patterns at home and in society; one person was in charge, responsible for all others, and the individual religious' role was one of dependent (often childlike) obedience. Rules and authority were unquestioned absolutes promulgated as vehicles to salvation; many are familiar with the maxim "If you keep the rule, the rule will keep you" which prevailed during their formation and early religious life.

The impact of familial and early religious training is not easily dismissed, so many religious struggle with personal identity while resolving authority issues. If she feels that she must please others (as women are socially conditioned to do), believing her self-worth is dependent upon acceptance by others, the woman religious' perception of those in leadership will reflect her insecurity. It is not surprising that some religious offered comments reminiscent of traditional feminine subservience. Said a thirty-seven-year-old religious, "I feared authority so much that I felt inferior even being near an authority person. Now at thirty-seven I still feel uncomfortable with authority persons because I feel inferior but the tension has lessened." A thirty-eight-year-old sister wrote, "[I] became less fearful of what those in charge would think of me."

Progressing beyond social conditioning generally led the religious to her "adolescence" in community. As she developed personally, and society developed corporately, blind adherence to a body of absolutes became increasingly suspect. Demanding autonomy and personal responsibility, many sisters entered a rebellious stage during which they asserted independence, questioning everything. Such a stage is evident in the remarks of the thirty-eight-year-old sister who said, "I first changed from accepting everything to being rebellious about the pettiness and unwillingness to change. I then changed— became more able to differentiate between legalism and essential obedience."

Recognizing the difference between "legalism and essential obedience" is the hallmark of a religious' adult status within community. No longer accepting authority for its own sake, but now realizing authority's role in the institutional structure, the woman religious who has "grown up" in community is more critically aware of the fallibility of persons, institutions, and structures. She demonstrates greater sensitivity to the human condition reflected in persons and their work—including persons in authority. Therefore, authority issues in midlife are not isolated crises emerging apart from the woman's overall development, but a culmination of personal and social growth issues.

Although both pre-midlife and midlife religious are cognizant of changing authority structures, the midlifer's awareness is qualitatively different because of her immersion in authority itself. The woman in her late thirties and early forties is no longer afforded the luxury of speculating and hypothesizing about alternative leadership styles apart from her active role in their actualization in community; no longer the "young sister" waiting to react to decisions from above, she is now the "decision maker"—the provincial, president, or council member of her community. Her responsibilities are greater, her position more central, and her overall involvement more intrinsically pervasive.[15] "I became a superior and remained one for twenty years," said a fifty-five-year-old; "I became convinced that authority is service—of unity, justice, love." Also speaking from personal experience, a forty-seven-year-old wrote, "As a superior I could not be responsible for others. I had to allow them to be responsible for themselves."

Perceptions of authority are culture-bound phenomena; religious who experienced both pre- and post-Vatican II authority models report a qualitatively different reaction to their midlife reassessment than will those who have known only the post-Vatican II community life-style. For contemporary religious, assuming adult, responsible, decision-making status in community closely paralleled assuming adult status in their families. In both cases, sisters needed to reconcile traditional training in respect and obedience with an emerging need for collaboration and responsibility.

Authority in Church

Consistent with the results reported for changing perceptions toward authority in the convent, 92 percent of women religious indicated a change in their perception toward authority in the Church. The most frequently reported age for the change was between thirty-five and forty, although many indicated a change of attitude prior to age thirty-five (41 percent).

Changes in both Church and society have undoubtedly combined to precipitate some of the altered perceptions, while emphasis on human liberation, espoused by those seeking full ministry for women in the Church, has also contributed to the diminution of the absolute authority of the institutional Church. Neither cultural transitions nor developmental psychology alone accounts for alterations in attitudes, yet women religious indicate that the key time for coping with changing perception is during midlife transition.

For many religious, questioning Church authority is bittersweet. Although appreciating their role as responsible Church members, some are angry and disappointed in themselves as well as Church leaders for creating expectations of absolute security and correctness.

I no longer accepted infallibility—recognized many errors, both traditionally, theologically and pastorally in the past and present. Came to be strong in my belief in the workings of God in all our lives, not just in the hierarchy's judgements, etc.   [age thirty-eight]

To question Church authority is, for many, to flirt with eternal damnation. They can risk restructuring family interactions, even though it is painful and seems to border on disrespect, and they will challenge community government, even though it flies in the face of centuries of tradition, but they hesitate to assess Church systems critically because of deeply rooted patriarchal training suggesting that ordained men are the embodiment of God on earth; to question them is to question God, to criticize them is to criticize God. Childhood fears combined with bad theology attributing supernatural status to ordained persons prohibit many from relinquishing juvenile notions about clergy and Church. The Church is perceived as sacred, as above and beyond the human institution composed of human persons that it is. Many religious who are willing to assume adult status in their families and to mature in community responsibility are reluctant to become adults ecclesiastically. It is difficult for them to accept that nothing human, not even the Church, is flawless.

Accepting the Church's hierarchical system as human and fallible is painful enough, but living with the institution's refusal to admit its weaknesses and alter its ways fans the fires of many angers. Frustration was voiced again and again by midlife religious who seek greater participatory involvement in ministry, decision making, and policy writing. One fifty-seven-year-old handles her dilemma from within the system: "I refuse to be co-opted by the system, yet I keep one foot in to help myself and them be honest. I work in the Chancery in the area of planning for implementation of shared responsibility." Another, forty years old, wrote, "I learned what the Church really should be—and chose to function within it on the level of community side by side—not top-down."

Sisters dissatisfied with authority and authority structures within their communities feel they can do something to effect change; they are less optimistic about their impact on the larger institution of the Church, which has traditionally minimized the person and role of women and, in some quarters, persists in its belief that women religious should be "dutiful daughters," ever respectful of the insights and largess of "concerned and protecting fathers." The question here is one more of systemic change than of midlife adjustment, yet midlife religious—who know that they are *not* children, *not* dutiful daughters, *not* second-class citizens—feel it with special poignancy.

They are increasingly willing to work toward reeducation and reorganization of Church structures, even if their efforts require unpopular stands. One superior, a forty-two-year-old woman, concluded, "We may be misunderstood and we may be disliked for it, but I and my community members will not work in parishes where we are not attributed adult status."

Women religious frustrated by contemporary Church structure and leadership are encouraged by their religious and lay sisters to persist in seeking change; Joan Ohanneson issues a strong exhortation in her book *Woman Survivor in the Church:*

> If, indeed, women religious are the most highly educated group of women in the world, then by virtue of profession, training, and access, they are the logical leaders of women in the church. By virtue of their professed commitment as religious women, they are received and accepted in church circles where laywomen are not even invited. While in the past, their energies in dealing with the hierarchy were understandably centered on recognition, reorganization, and renewal in regard to their religious communities, now there is a new agenda which reflects the feminist consciousness and which demands attention. In light of that consciousness, for women religious to limit their qualities of leadership to the confines of community life is to deny their gifts to all people, as well as to reinforce the elitist concept of religious life which has drained so much of the church's creative energy for so long.[16]

Social changes as well as adult identity have brought contemporary women religious to an acute moment in ecclesial policy-making. Through their midlife interiorization, yielding a strong sense of self and respect for their womanhood, religious can apply their insights, skills, and dissatisfactions to challenge institutions which need them—whether they realize it or not—to effect a more just future for those inside of and outside of the Church. The future of these ambitions is uncertain, but one fact remains: sisters today now have the requisite tools to make a big—and necessary—difference.

Authority in government

Just as the woman in midlife reassesses her attitudes toward conventual and Church authority, so also does she reassess her attitudes toward authority in government. Seventy-nine percent of women religious reported an attitude shift toward government authority figures, and the most frequently reported age for the shift was between thirty-five and forty, again confirming the midlife literature which predicts such attitudinal shifts during midlife transition.

As in all other authority structures discussed so far, altering perceptions of governmental authority is a multifacted phenomenon. The breakdown of patriotic solidarity resulting from a more truthful perception of war and of our part in it following the Vietnam conflict, a more realistic perception of politicians following the dishonorable events of Watergate, and the continual press reporting of flagrant misconduct of government officials: these forces coalesced with an emerging emphasis on personal responsibility to diminish unqualified respect for and simplistic confidence in government structure and governmental leadership. Traditionally, women religious were not active in government affairs and, like most citizens, were not particularly aware of political activities. Today, because of agencies such as Network, a lobby of religious women of many communities, Common Cause, Ground Zero, and the many groups devoted to social justice, as well as heightened consciousness regarding legislative issues, religious are more aware of and more actively involved in politics, lobbying, and legal issues.

> I always saw government as good until I began working in poor areas, then I saw nothing but red tape. I now have little faith in government.
> [age thirty-five]

> Recently I am attempting to deal with my cynicism regarding government. I expect much but trust little those in government. Hoping to grow in this area—more tolerant of human limits. [age thirty-seven]

> The poor and the havoc government wreaks in their lives disturbs me. I love this country, but I see its warts!   [age fifty]

Questioning of governmental authority is precipitated by the same dynamics as those involved in questioning community and Church authority. Social changes, new psychological insights, and personally maturing wisdom combine to elicit incisive reassessment and constructive criticism. Religious today are freer than their foremothers to become political activists, but the desire to do so, and the need upon which it is based, is often the result of midlife interiorization exploring personal and corporate destructiveness. One forty-year-old sister summarized the comments of many when she said,

> There is a growing urgency in our need to respond to unjust governments, including our own. "Separation of Church and State" is an untenable excuse for us to remain uninvolved, tacitly approving oppression. Donovan, Clark, Kazel, and Ford [the four women missionaries martyred in El Salvador] were not accidents! They were not radical youngsters; they were not left-wing agitators. And you know, three of them were in midlife!

Women religious clearly do experience an attitude change toward authority in their families, communities, Church, and government as part of their midlife transition. Their experiences are obviously quite different from men's, so they deal with issues in their own way with their own unique talents and insights. Maturing into midlife, the woman abandons many absolutes—including her childlike identity—as she confronts the arbitrariness of much authority and many authority structures. The process can be tumultuous and painful; one superior remarked, "I have to explain my reasons again and again to those around forty. They never seem satisfied with my explanations, especially if they don't agree with me." Becoming an authority figure herself, the woman religious learns that ideals and actualities do not easily meld; she is challenged to deeper understandings of human limitations while continuing her efforts to correct injustices. No longer young, not yet old, she realizes that she, the midlife woman religious, commands the future.

---

1. Hurlock, *Developmental Psychology*, especially chaps. 11 and 12.
2. The parent-child conflict of middle age is reviewed in most developmental psychology texts.
3. Levinson, *Seasons of a Man's Life*.

4. Rivers, Barnett, and Baruch, *How Women Grow, Learn, and Thrive.* Examples in this section are taken from this book, which is a well-written compilation of research findings relevant to male and female development.
5. Ibid., especially chap. 5.
6. Hyde and Rosenberg, *Half the Human Experience*, especially chap. 6.
7. Ibid., p. 96.
8. Nancy Friday, *My Mother, Myself* (New York: Delacorte Press, 1977).
9. Kolbenschlag, *Kiss Sleeping Beauty Good-Bye*; see chap. 2, "Snow White and Her Shadow."
10. Janet Ruffing, "Mother-Daughter Remnants in Religious Life," *Human Development* 3, no. 2 (1982): 46-54, p. 46.
11. Levinson, *Seasons of a Man's Life.*
12. See James Gill, "The Stresses of Leadership," *Human Development* 1, no. 1 (1980): 19-27.
13. See Gregory Manly, "Realistic Community Expectations," *Human Development* 2, no. 2 (1981): 34-38.
14. See Maslow's works, especially *Toward a Psychology of Being.*
15. See the interview with Eileen Kelly, S.S.A., in "Learning through Leadership," *Human Development* 1, no. 3 (1980): 6-13.
16. Ohanneson, *Woman Survivor in the Church*, pp. 85-86.

Chapter 5

Commitments reconsidered:
Midlife vocational adjustments

A major symptom of midlife transition turmoil is vocational and career dissatisfaction encompassing a reevaluation of life-style as well as professional involvement. Dramatic changes often occur, including radical career shifts and vocational reconsiderations. A complex and comprehensive midlife symptom, it can better be understood in the experience of the woman religious in comparison to its significance in the midlife transitions of three major population groups: married women, single women, and married men. All have unique vocational/career crises during midlife transition, and women religious' experiences are similar to all but identical to none of them.

Between 95 and 98 percent of all Americans marry,[1] and until recently, the roles assumed by each spouse were clearly known and well-delineated. The man was the economic provider; the woman was the homemaker. The young girl was raised understanding that her primary role in life was to marry and to bear children; thus, she was responsible for assuring fulfillment of that singular destiny, especially for making herself attractive—marketable—to a member of the opposite sex;[2] this is the femininity-achievement incompatibility referred to earlier. She was led to believe it unwise to invest too much time or energy in developing a career because (1) she did not want to be better educated or more competent than the men she would meet, and (2) she would be unable to realize her investment because she would, when married, abandon her career to pursue family responsibilities. Of course, some engaged in contingency planning, that is, pursued training in a traditional "woman's field" like teaching or nursing to secure income until they married or to provide a salary in the horrid event that they never married. However, such preparation was a stopgap measure—a safety precaution—to tide them over until the most important event of their lives, marriage, occurred.

To facilitate the transition from single to married status, the young woman was implicitly and often explicitly encouraged to suspend resolution of her adolescent identity task until she married, at which time she would assume her husband's identity, supporting him in his vocational aspirations and career ambitions. In this merger, the woman "did for" her husband to advance "their" careers; the husband's success became her success. Ready to relocate geographically for the sake of a promotion, willing to spend time with the children for the sake of division of labor, and primed to support her husband through the vicissitudes of his career, the woman accepted the domestic role as her destiny. No other role was modeled with approbation, none other was honored with "normalcy." Recall that Erikson attributed woman's "natural proclivity" for domestic and nurturing tasks to her internally located uterus.

For the woman who grew up in this sociocultural environment, midlife transition is a painful awakening to the fact that she has lived vicariously; that she has attempted to use her life to enhance the lives of others without having first established a solid base for such giving in the assessment and ownership of her own talents and strengths. Operating from an undiscovered, unaffirmed base, many women use the lives of their children and husbands to achieve a semblance of meaning in their own lives. They, therefore, do not really enhance the lives of family members as they could if they were operating from a foundation of self-worth apart from the worth of another. By midlife, a woman's children are grown and independent, leaving her with little to do around the house; her husband, immersed as before in his career and vocational concerns, seems increasingly distant from her. Disenchanted with living vicariously through children and husband, the woman begins to question herself—*her* goals, *her* ambitions, *her* meaning in life—and begins to suspect, perhaps for the first time in her life, an identity unique to herself.

She may want to return to college or to enter the work world, but senses that both options are dependent upon her husband's approval or ability to finance the endeavor.[3] Misunderstandings may emerge as the woman moves forward to develop academic and professional skills and the man challenges both the necessity and feasibility of such a move. Disappointed, the woman may question her past dedication to this man and his goals, her role in the relationship, and her reasons for remaining in it.

However, even if she enjoys the support of her spouse in establishing a second career, the midlife married woman is discouraged to learn that it is more difficult for her to obtain employment and promotions than it is for a man.[4] Her options, because of lack of experience as well as time away from the work arena, are limited primarily to low-paying clerical jobs or to traditional "women's work" in education, health care, or cosmetology, low-paying, low-status jobs because of minimal competition from men.[5]

Job satisfaction and career success are generally lower for women than for men because women are unable to procure employment and remuneration commensurate with their training and ability. The woman's sense of worth is further diminished by a husband who "humors" or "tolerates" her ventures into the marketplace, reminding her that she need not endure these frustrations because his income is adequate for both of them. The combination of vocational frustration and patronizing support can culminate in marital discord and even divorce as the woman strives to discover her own identity.

The single woman encounters many of the same frustrations as the married woman in addition to some indigenous to her unique status in society. Vocational successes are seldom commensurate with ability and experience, even if the woman has been in the work force since early adulthood. Hurlock notes, "This failure [to achieve success] is due not to a lack of ability and training but to prejudice against women in positions of responsibility."[6] Likewise, career satisfactions are also lower for women than for men because of untapped skills and reduced salaries, all of which are compounded by resentment over not receiving promotions and pay increases when deserved. If a middle-aged woman loses her job, she is less likely than a middle-aged man to find other employment; she must sometimes take a premature retirement because of policy or prejudice or both.

The frustrations of limited career opportunities force many single women to change jobs or even careers, and as their economic future becomes increasingly bleak because of limited chances for advancement, they may begin to question the wisdom of their decisions, made much earlier in life, to remain single and to pursue a career. Realizing that their childbearing years are rapidly diminishing, they may begin to yearn for the assumed closeness and security of a marital relationship. As a woman passes forty, her chances for marriage become markedly slimmer, more so for the single woman than for the divorced or widowed woman.[7] She may feel desperate, trapped, mistreated, and misunderstood, believing that her time and chances are running out, that she must restructure quickly if she is to make a difference in her life and her future. She acts with a sense of urgency, desperation, and often anger, sensing her plight as unjust payment exacted for remaining part of the 2 to 5 percent of the female population who do not opt for society's preferred role for the woman as wife and mother.

Paradoxically, the career/vocational reevaluations of the midlife transition for both married and single women generate an appreciation—sometimes false in its simplistic nature—of the other's way of life; the married woman envies the single woman's freedom and apparent career stability whereas the single woman envies the married woman's apparent emotional security. Blind to the realities of the other's predicament, each assumes that the other's life-style might provide the vehicle for actualization as she strives to establish a sense of identity apart from her marriage or career.[8] Neither has the career possibilities of either married or single men, and the resulting anger can compound the midlife frustration already engendered.

The man, whether married or single, is encouraged by the sociocultural milieu to establish a sense of self and purpose as he resolves his adolescent identity crisis. Rising to this expectation, the man develops himself through his family as well as through his career. He selects a job or profession that will allow him to actualize himself, challenging his skills and utilizing his potentials as a contributing member of society. He also selects a wife, a person to share his dreams and visions and to assist him in the realization of his goals. In exchange for her dedication, he supports her and the children.[9] It is important to note the difference between men's and women's perception of the married life-style. For the woman, marriage—securing a mate—*is* her goal; it is her achievement and, as such, is an end point often realized, for the most part, by the time she is in her midtwenties. If she considers work or career at all, it is usually as ancillary to the *real* business of being married. It is not surprising, then, that the woman's focus, activities, and energies are directed toward the family unit and its involvements, and her dedication to vicarious living through this unit becomes understandable in light of societal expectations.

For the man, marriage is *part* of his identity and often a *vehicle* for realizing that identity, but it is seldom the embodiment of the totality of his sense of self that it is for the woman. The man certainly values his family and the inherent support generated by a spouse who is willing to do everything possible to advance his ambitions and share his disappointments, but he seldom attributes the importance to family that he assigns to career. For the man, career must be worked at and worked on while marriage and family tend to "be there."

As he approaches his forties, he begins to question all that he has worked for; the questioning is as much the result of midlife restlessness as it is the result of realities in his work. He generally finds that he has advanced as far as he can within his career and is frustrated as younger, more ambitious men are promoted over him. Confused and frightened, he searches for reasons, often projecting onto his family, superiors, and institutions, blaming them for his lack of upward mobility and success at this, the prime of his professional life. Even if successful, however, he feels hollow about his achievements and begins to question their value and worth.

Oppressed by the feeling that time is running out ("After all," he reasons, "I'm getting too old to be marketable"), he operates out of a sense of immediacy, an imperative that something be done right away before it is too late. He has three options now: (1) he can recommit himself to his profession, working longer and harder to prove to himself and to others that he is still a very capable employee and definitely deserving of further promotions and pay raises; (2) he can change jobs or even careers;[10] or (3) he can resign himself to the reality of his career status, tolerating the necessary tedium for the sake of income, while investing time and energy in more rewarding, exciting hobbies and avocations.[11] His freedom to select any of these options is often seriously hampered by familial obligations which, by this time, include house payments, college tuition payments, and general family maintenance. To move may be unrealistic, especially if he doubts his ability to find new employment or relocate satisfactorily.

His dilemma is philosophical as well as pragmatic as he questions the motivations that led him to this current plight. He must deal with his unrealized ambitions and hopes, accepting that some of his youthful aspirations were tinged with an adolescent idealism which he had failed to nurture through the years. Disappointed because he has not accomplished his dreams and embarrassed because these dreams were somewhat unrealistic, he attempts to reconcile his current situation with his past aspirations.[12]

Often succumbing to the "If only..." syndrome, he plays the blaming game. To his wife he complains that *she* is responsible for his unhappiness and misery: "If only you had agreed to move to the West Coast when that opening came up...," "If only you hadn't encouraged me to spend so much time on that project...," "If only you hadn't insisted on college for all the kids...." With regard to his superiors, he deludes himself with the idea that *they* deliberately conspired to minimize his career potential: "If only you hadn't talked me into that move...," "If only you had been more sensitive to my expertise...," "If only you weren't so concerned about profits...." Operating more out of his need for intrapersonal order than out of a need to hurt others deliberately, the midlife man searches for a solution to his career problems, a career through which he has probably derived considerable self-esteem.

He feels hurt and misunderstood as he faces an uncomprehending wife reacting out of her *own* hurt from his criticisms. He is baffled by her insistence that she begin work on her own education and career, interpreting this stance as further evidence of his failure as a provider. He begins to resent the restrictions imposed on him by marriage and family, suspecting that he could have become the man he had always hoped to be if it were not for his wife and children and their demands on him. Resenting his superiors and institutions as though they had conspired to restrict his advancements, he fantasizes great acceptance and adulation from other employers in other institutions he might have joined if only he had been free to make the move.

Another tension during the career/vocational midlife reassessment is the disintegration of the mentoring relationship that developed earlier in the man's career. Much more common among men than women, the mentoring relationship is a unique bond between an older, more experienced professional and a younger, talented, promising new worker.[13] Neither a father figure nor a friend, but a little of each, the mentor takes special interest in the skills and advancements of the younger man, arranging promotions, educating him, and adjusting assignments so that "his man" has opportunities for recognition in his work. As the midlifer begins to reap the benefits of his mentor's efforts, he might come into direct conflict and competition with him, desiring his mentor's position but reluctant to dethrone the very person responsible for his advancement. Unable to work *with* his mentor, but no longer able to work *under* him, the midlifer in transition must sever his ties to pursue advancement on his own merits and skills. The hostilities resulting from this split are difficult for the mentor as well as for the protégé, creating hurt feelings and misunderstandings on both sides. To relieve the tensions, many men change jobs or even relocate geographically.

All three groups—married women, single women, and married men—experience upheaval in their life-styles in an effort to integrate earlier life ambitions with present realities. They are angry with themselves for having allowed a younger "other self" to presumptuously conclude far-reaching and significant life decisions; they are angry at others for encouraging that other self in such rashness. "The grass is greener" syndrome is pervasive as all three groups consider alternatives and weigh possibilities. The woman religious struggling with her personal ruminations during interiorization experiences the upheaval felt by all three major groups as well as some symptoms unique to her style of life.

In her career-oriented, celibate but communal life-style, the woman religious reports experiences common to all three groups. Like the married woman, she has devoted her life and energy to the service of others and done so in a preestablished pattern, often before she has identified the nature of the energy she is contributing. Although the woman religious does not merge her identity totally with another, deriving vicarious satisfaction from the successes of the other, she does adopt the identity of a community and the community's unique charism and apostolate and builds her life around them. Like her married sister who delayed developing her personal identity until meeting a man whose identity she could assume, the woman religious forestalled her personal identity search as she learned to accept the identity of her community.

> The transference of a symbiotic style of relationship to one's religious community is common, especially among younger women. During the initial stages of formation and the first few years of ministry, we tend to become identified with the community. Our partnership relationship is with the congregation as we adapt to its life and ministry.[14]

As she enters midlife, the religious, like her married sister, wonders what her identity would be like apart from her commitment to this community. Such thinking is risky because it implies tacit rejection, at least for the duration of the questioning, of the identity base from which the midlife wanderer has operated for so long. Ruffing maintains that this questioning is necessary for the full development of personhood among woman religious: "Eventually, however, if we are to become fully self-actualized women, we will find it necessary to separate our personal identity from submersion in the group."[15]

This is not to suggest that the midlife religious or her married sisters deliberately opted to be less than they were capable of being by forestalling personal identity formation for "other identity" during their adolescent decision-making. These women were products of their cultures, never thinking that their development was inferior to that of men. Many sisters, after hearing this discussion, respond indignantly that they *did*, in fact, work very diligently to formulate what they believed to be an identity—the identity of a good, dedicated, committed religious. This is true! But careful analysis of the assumptions underlying traditional definitions of "good sisters" and "good wives" reveals the bias that personality formation—for women—was dependent upon adherence to externally based norms established by others rather than internally based ideals flowing from a well-researched sense of self. It is during the interiorization of the midlife transition that many women come to realize the disparities between what they thought constituted personal identity and what they now *know* to be their identity.

As she begins to formulate an identity of her own, the midlife wanderer appeals to the community for financial support of a new vocational endeavor, and, like her homemaker sister who is angry and hurt when her husband refuses to fund her ambitions after "all she has done for him," the midlife religious becomes angry with her community administration if it cannot or will not finance her requests after "all she has done for them."

Like her single sister who has dedicated her life to a special ideal or goal and who later discovers that her achievements and satisfactions are restricted by the type of work she is in ("women's work") or by societal prejudices, the woman religious questions the validity of her earlier decisions, especially celibacy, and supposes she might feel more fulfilled if she were in an intimate marital relationship in addition to or apart from her career involvements. This is, of course, made more immediate by the reality of physical aging which imposes a predetermined limit on childbearing ability.

Like her career-oriented married brother, the woman religious has learned to derive considerable self-esteem from her work. When she finds this no longer satisfying, she lashes out at those persons and institutions that she perceives to stand in the way of her advancement. She would like to try new work or even new locations but is impeded by community restrictions or limited apostolic opportunities. Just as men frustrated by lack of professional advancement project blame for their perceived failures onto their families and institutions, so also do women religious blame their communities, schools, and church for restricting their ambitions and precluding success options.

Women religious are more likely to experience mentoring relationships than are their married and single sisters because of their immersion in all-female work situations such as schools and hospitals, which are traditionally populated by nuns who have both a personal and a community investment in the futures of these institutions. Of course, this imposes the additional burden for the woman religious in midlife of terminating or modifying mentoring relationships, that is, severing ties from superiors and older sisters who have taken a special interest in her religious and professional development. The conflicts are painful and the woman religious, unlike the career man, is not always free to change jobs or seek geographic relocation; she must continue to live closely with those from whom she has distanced herself psychologically and emotionally. Even if she has surpassed her religious mentors in areas of achievement and understanding, she feels bound by the community life system to remain beholden to their dispositions and decisions and, consequently, may not attain the psychological independence available to males in comparable situations.

> My first superior gave me every break in the book. She helped me with my classes and extended privileges like shopping and visiting. I did well; my teaching improved and my disposition flourished! But now I see what was happening. She ignored some women who really needed help—and others who threatened her—to make me her shining light before the community. Now she insists that I spend time with her and support her position at community meetings—something I can't really do—out of "loyalty" to all she gave me. I don't agree with her but I can't escape her.   [age forty-nine]

The woman religious, like her lay sisters, has only recently become aware of and been permitted to consider and pursue life-styles and careers beyond the traditional options of large-group living and educational/medical work. These recent options, though exciting and liberating, are somewhat limited by their newness as well as by long-standing stereotypes regarding women and their inability to handle themselves in certain areas of work.

As seems evident, the problem is neither strictly career nor exclusively vocational; both profession and life-style are interwoven into the complex web of what a person does and how she does it, so that turmoil in one sphere almost automatically is echoed by turmoil in the other. The midlifer feels her time running out; her vocational/career questions assume a desperation and immediacy that compound and heighten the confusion. In attempting to resolve the conflicts, the midlife religious and her superiors are often distracted by arguing and misunderstanding, digressing away from the core of the matter, namely, a much more pervasive disgruntlement with self and life. Furthermore, the male-dominated Church, which imposes even greater vocational restrictions on women than does society at large, becomes another target—and possible distraction—for the midlife religious in transition.

The importance of the career-change factor for women religious in midlife is evident in the statistic that 75 percent of those surveyed made a career change, with the peak time for doing so being between thirty-five and forty years of age. Some sisters indicated that they made their career changes at the request of their community administration while others reported that they initiated changes themselves. Because religious have only recently been permitted to consider work other than the community's established apostolate, it is highly likely that as many changed careers in response to this option as changed because of midlife restlessness. The emergence of greater career choice for women religious as a recent phenomenon is reflected in the fact that 60 percent of women religious indicated that they pursued their highest academic degree out of personal choice. Most sisters began work on their highest degree before they were thirty. Nevertheless, 48 percent returned to school after age thirty, and all of these did so out of personal choice. It is highly likely that more sisters will choose to pursue advanced degrees at later ages (after thirty) than before as past restrictions on religious' career options are lifted.

Reasons for changing careers were multifaceted. Some reported that they were never very interested in the community's established apostolate in the first place, but were attracted to the community and therefore were willing to assume the work as "part of the package"; given the option to pursue something different, they welcomed and responded to the opportunity. Said a forty-eight-year-old, "I couldn't take teaching any longer; I was *busy* but very bored."

Many career changes were the result of suggestions or requests from either community or parish administrators; that so many waited for an externally based impetus is probably reflective of traditional conventual living and social conditioning more than a reluctance to change. Only future research with sisters who have grown up in post-Vatican II religious life-styles can determine the extent to which they feel free to suggest their own career revisions.[16]

Philosophical inconsistencies motivated some to seek new careers. A forty-five-year-old religious explained her philosophical reasons for going *into* religious education:

> I really went from the daily classroom to religious education because I felt kids in the daily classroom weren't in Catholic school for the right reason. I wanted to work with those who really wanted faith life. From religious education work I got into a lot of pastoral work and now I do that full time.

By contrast, a thirty-eight-year-old *left* religious education. But she, too, had a philosophical basis for her move:

> I terminated my position as a parish religious education coordinator because I could no longer in conscience say the things that I "had to say as an official church person." I also minded the oppression of the male hierarchy.

Technological change, diversified interests, and the increased availability of education have combined in contemporary society to make the one-career-per-lifetime belief a myth. Research indicates that most workers, men and women alike, can expect to have two or more careers during their adult lives, and women religious are no exception. Therefore, some sought career changes because they were finding themselves increasingly ineffective in their first careers. "I left education because there was too much conflict for too little return," wrote a thirty-nine-year-old sister. She, like many of her sisters, fully expected to remain in education throughout her productive years; her realization that she was disenchanted with her job after fifteen years of successful employment both surprised and frightened her. She initially blamed herself for her dissatisfaction, thinking she had done something wrong to diminish her earlier effectiveness. She tried many new approaches, participated in workshops, and registered for some courses in a nearby college to bolster her enthusiasm—all to no avail. When her disgruntlement became intolerable during her midlife transition, she sought further education and changed jobs.

Even if she remains in her original occupation during and after her transition, the midlife wanderer discovers that she is somehow different in her job. She might change her style, she might redirect the focus of her energy, or she might rededicate herself to earlier-espoused commitments. Whatever her reasons for staying in her job, she is different as a result of her midlife reassessment.

Married persons often blame their marriages for midlife discomfort; single persons blame their singleness. It is not suprising, then, that the women religious surveyed blamed their life-style and 58 percent of them considered leaving the convent.

Those who reported vocational crises indicated two major periods of questioning: the late twenties (usually prior to final vows) and the late thirties (during their midlife transitions). Those who identified two periods of doubt specified the second upheaval as the more painful and serious of the two.

Religious who reassess vocation as part of their midlife transition do so for a variety of complex and interdependent reasons. Like their married sisters who perceived marriage as a goal in itself, some religious viewed "being a nun" as their end point in life; once they took final vows they were mystified to discover that simply "being in a state" was insufficient satisfaction because they—like their married sisters—had never formulated a personal identity apart from their status as "nun."

Some question the feasibility of remaining celibate; they would like to marry and they feel hampered by their commitment to community life-style from exploring this option. Others question their ability to maintain their credibility regarding human liberation and justice issues while participating actively in a system that seems to do little more than pay lip service to these concerns. One sister said, "I buy so little of the orthodox position of the Church that I wonder how long I can remain formally associated with it. I *want* and need community life, but am increasingly convinced I'm being a hypocrite." Others question the extent to which they can pursue career aspirations while remaining in community.

> Now that we have so many more options I would love to go into medicine. But the costs are so high—community just can't support me while I drop out of my current job (I'm paid well) to go to med school. Especially at my age. Sometimes I think I should just leave and do it on my own, even though I don't want to.   [age thirty-nine]

Some addressed an oppression in community living which they sensed more keenly during their midlife transitions. Explained one,

> When I was twenty I was the "young sister" and was expected to provide the manual labor and entertainment that traditionally went with the title. When I was thirty-nine, I was still being called the "young sister" and still being expected to fulfill all those functions. Enough is enough. I don't mind doing my share, but it was the *expectation* that was getting to me; it was like they *assumed* I loved doing all those things. I went through a lot of guilt until I finally worked it out for myself. And I'll admit, I almost left because of it.
> [age forty-three]

Seeking space and time to work through their community-living concerns, some sisters find release in opting for either a smaller or larger living situation, depending on their particular needs. In this respect, religious have an advantage over their married contemporaries who would probably like to take a "leave of absence" from their families but cannot. Furthermore, sisters can combine their needs for career change and solitude by requesting a year for study in an out-of-town university.

> I chose to get my master's degree in a place where I knew no one— needed to "prove" to myself that I could make it—make it socially, intellectually, emotionally, psychologically, spiritually on my own. It was a *very good experience.*   [age thirty-eight]

Forty-five percent of women religious indicated a desire to be away from community, either officially (via *ex claustration*) or unofficially (via study or a private apartment) for six months or longer. Of those, 56 percent acted on their desire, with the most frequently reported age for this move being between thirty-five and forty. It is possible that many remained in community because they had the opportunity to experience a change of scenery and pace while struggling with midlife upsets; there is no way of knowing how many eventually left community because of or in spite of such experience.

Some, because of their personal identity formation during midlife, discover that their "new self" is incompatible with their "community self"—the identity to which they had subscribed for so many years. In some cases, women religious can reconcile the inconsistencies and remain comfortably and honestly in community; others cannot.

The reasons for leaving community are as numerous and complex as the reasons for entering it. One fact emerges, however: vocational crises tend to erupt with vehemence during midlife transition.

Intimacy in midlife

Intimacy issues are an intricate facet of midlife vocational/career reassessments as well as the midlife transition in general. Typically a lonely time, a time of experiencing isolation and alienation, the midlife transition magnifies the need for close, meaningful relationships in which the woman can share her pain and insights, affirm her uniqueness in her emerging identity, and enjoy the satisfaction of extending beyond herself as she attempts to maintain contact with others.

A comprehensive analysis of relationships and intimacy is beyond the scope of this discussion, but a few general comments on the development of relationships as well as the development of relationships in religious life lend understanding to the midlife wanderer's conflicts.

A major task of early adulthood is to establish a variety of acquaintances and friends with and through whom a woman can develop her social/emotional skills. To be accepted and to be part of the group is a necessary healthy human need that precedes full actualization.[17] Pleasing others, anticipating and meeting their desires, and developing a constellation of friends are valid activities for the maturing woman in early adulthood.

Although necessary, these relationships are not ultimately satisfying; they are "busy," superficial, task-oriented, and, consequently, do not meet the more basic human need to be deeply understood and deeply accepted, a longing that emerges after the general friendship needs characteristic of early adulthood are met.

The adult developmental trend away from many to fewer but deeper relationships is reflected in these comments:

From twenty to twenty-five, I valued being liked by peers, others. Up through my early thirties, it was important knowing that my friendships were mutual, knowing that my friends felt secure in our relationship.   [age thirty-two]

Being accepted was most important in my early twenties. Now, at thirty-six, I prefer fewer relationships that have depth rather than a number of acquaintances.   [age thirty-six]

From twenty to twenty-five I was moody and pretty closed because of my poor self-concept. My interpersonal relationships were so shallow that all I hoped for was that others would like me. Now I am very lucky to have a very faithful friend with whom I share deeply in all areas.
                                                                    [age thirty-seven]

In my early twenties, I valued the number of friendships; wanted many friends. In my late twenties I sought exclusiveness with a few—rather immature, very ambivalent, possessive. In my late thirties I seek greater intimacy with fewer people but have greater appreciation for many.   [age forty]

During my early twenties it was important to be friendly, to have others be friendly to me; to chat and be rather casual but not too close. I then moved to fewer friends but much deeper relationships, quality time rather than quantity (late twenties). Many of these friends are still part of my life today. Now (forties), I'm much more choosey with friendship, realizing there are some people who just aren't for me or I for them. I can better accept people but not choose to be extremely close to them.   [age forty-five]

Intrapersonal and interpersonal growth are interdependent developments; only by cultivating a firmer, deeper sense of self can the woman enter into meaningful communication with and reflect reverence for another equally profound self. Growing in personal awareness, including awareness of physical, intellectual, emotional, and spiritual aspects, she becomes increasingly cognizant of her ultimate aloneness and profoundly sensitive to her need for self-transcendence actualized through relationship. The process is continuous, developmental, and dynamic; hence, relationships that were satisfying during adolescence wane in early adulthood; likewise, the relationship systems of early adulthood prove inadequate for the needs of midlife.

The progression from childhood to adulthood is characterized by the increasing ability to establish a balance between self- and other-directed growth. Becoming less dependent on the approval of others for a personal sense of esteem without becoming egocentric and insensitive is a lifelong task involving mistakes, pain, and elation as the individual experiences integration both within and outside of relationship. Direct confrontation of the attachment/separateness polarity, as elaborated earlier, is a major task of the midlife transition dealing with this very tension.

Awakening to a profound sense of self normally occurs through infatuation, that total immersion in another that alerts the individual to her worth as a person unique to herself yet capable of complete understanding, acceptance, and reverence for another. It is necessary experience, an essential condition for human as well as spiritual growth,[18] which can occur at any time in life but generally occurs in adolescence or early adulthood. Infatuation is so pervasive an experience that it affects all aspects of being—physical, emotional, intellectual, social, and spiritual—and as such, can generate sexual interests and desires and can precipitate acting on these desires.

Some persons, because of their religious mores or personal fears, do not allow themselves to risk infatuation with its potential for sexual involvement; consequently, they block their own development. Intimacy needs that are "taken to the Lord" as the woman runs pell-mell from other people will remain forever frustrated; grace builds on nature, including the nature of two persons growing and struggling through an intimate relationship. "There is a curious tendency by many Christians to idealize intimacy with God and demean intimacy with their fellow humans."[19] Taking intimacy problems to God might save the woman the agony of sexual threat, but it diminishes her growth as a human destined to interact with others while it also diminishes the quality of her prayer and her relationship with her God.

Pre-Vatican II religious life-styles reflected the Church's heritage of spiritual dualism (spirit over matter) and patriarchal dualism (man over woman).[20] These philosophical attitudes perceived the body as a necessary evil to be disciplined and tolerated for the sake of heavenly rewards while simultaneously projecting all fears of sexuality and intimacy onto women and their symbolic fecundity and seductiveness. Close personal relationships were to be avoided lest the individuals involved be tempted beyond their ability to resist. Women religious were taught to keep a distance from other women religious as well as from men, and were imbued with extraordinary fears of their own bodies and emotions. The onus of "particular friendships," well-entrenched in the background of every religious, was taught from the concept that their exclusivity had no place in community; the more truthful, underlying reason was the fear of sexual acting out within the context of intimacy. The culmination of years of prohibition more often resulted in curiousity and titillation—if not reactive repression—than control, and distorted the definition of intimacy. Intimacy and sexuality were thus treated as synonymous, an unfortunate association that deprived many religious of valuable opportunities for dynamic human and spiritual growth, because *all* growth is one. Intimacy is a prerequisite for spiritual development; to deny it is to deny growth, to preclude the Divine from manifesting another precious segment of eternity-on-earth.

A major problem confounding the intimacy needs of midlife is this Judeo-Christian proclivity for confusing intimacy and genital sexuality. Married, single, and religious persons are often victims of this pervasive erroneous assumption and, consequently, believe that only through sexuality can they meet intimacy needs.

It is no surprise, then, that one of the most highly popularized symptoms of the midlife transition is the extramarital affair.[21] Reasons for pursuing affairs, given by men and women alike, are multifaceted: to prove desirability, to prove femininity or masculinity, to establish intimacy, or to prove personal independence. Although sexual behavior and sexual release may be a component of the extramarital intrigues, clandestine liaisons are often pursued for purposes other than sexual satisfaction. In fact, one couple meeting secretly for more than a year confessed that they had never had intercourse—and did not want to; they were satisfied just knowing that the other cared and that they had "put one over" on their spouses! Those involved in extramarital affairs often explain their behavior as resulting from insensitive treatment at home: "My wife just nags and nags about what I'm *not* getting done; my friend makes me feel good for what I *am* getting done. I feel like a man when I'm with her." Or "My husband treats me like a commodity—a live-in maid. My friend treats me like a woman—like a person who can think and has feelings."

Parallel types of statements are sometimes made by religious who are involved in intense relationships, for example, "If community would be more sensitive to me and my needs, I wouldn't feel driven to seek affirmation this way." Or, "I feel like such a person when I'm with him; I feel I'm just a number in community."

Although sexual concerns are seldom the sole reason for extra-marital involvements, it would be naive to rule them out completely since they are the cause of much marital as well as vocational discord in midlife.[22] The difficulties stem from many sources and are not limited to married persons alone.[23]

First of all, the timetable for peak sexual interest and drive is different for men and women,[24] with the man's drive peaking in early adulthood and the woman's peaking in her thirties and later. Second, women tend to lose their sexual inhibitions as they age and become more actively interested in sexual activities. Third, married women (and single women involved in affairs) tend to let their husbands (partners) dictate the frequency and style of sexual interchange and become frustrated as their husbands' (partners') interest wanes. Fourth, couples who have failed to nurture their relationships throughout the years of marriage (or an affair) often discover emptiness—a need for intimacy—which they try to recover in the bedroom without first talking through their difficulties or reacquainting themselves with each other. As sex alone does not guarantee intimacy, the resulting frustrations further delude them into blaming their sex life for the deteriorating interpersonal relationship. The intimacy-sexuality confusions are not limited to married or lay persons; religious are also vulnerable to them.

The juxtaposition of increased intimacy needs, increased sexual interest, and reduced sexual inhibitions precipitates serious dilemmas for the midlife woman religious who is struggling with loneliness, career dissatisfaction, and vocational doubts. As she matures, the woman religious, like her lay sister, develops a greater appreciation for close, meaningful relationships with persons of both sexes.[25] In her youth, she was interested in impressing others and being accepted by many; in her more mature years, she values quality more than quantity. Coping with changing relationship values, she becomes vulnerable to infatuation and its concomitant immersion in another, especially if she has denied herself experiences of infatuation in her youth. The pressures that mount through years of denial, repression, and unrealistic dichotomies between intimacy and sexuality may, in the search for meaningful intimacy, culminate in a greater willingness to risk violation of past taboos for the sake of present affectionate expressions.

Community living does not exempt the woman religious from the developmental processes experienced by her lay sisters; 95 percent of women religious report an increase in sexual interests and desires which becomes markedly pronounced between the ages of thirty-five and forty but which is notably strong during both the early thirties and early forties. Since most religious were not prepared for this normal, predictable, natural psychological phenomenon, they were amazed and frightened at its occurrence. Dealing with such feelings is difficult under the healthiest of circumstances, but is proportionately more difficult for persons who know little or nothing of their psychological development and their sexual/affectionate selves. Reactions ranged from self-blame to curiosity to despair. "Is this a sign that I can no longer live celibacy?" "Have I failed in my prayer life somehow?" "Perhaps I'm neglecting my vocation." Such reasons might be *part* of the phenomenon of increased sexual desires in midlife but never suffice as singular cause-effect explanations.

Feelings and thoughts about sex are as normal a part of being alive and human as are feelings and thoughts about food, relationship, rest, relaxation, recreation, and intellectual stimulation. However, years of repression, denial, and ignorance about sex and sexual matters create a vacuum in self-awareness, resulting in a personality hiatus in which the midlife wanderer is an adult in most areas of her life but a child in her sexual self-knowledge and self-awareness. Her sexually stunted self is ill prepared to deal with a normal adult developmental occurrence and, like a child confronted by a frightening and new experience, she is caught in an approach-avoidance conflict. Desiring to know more about this fascinating preoccupation, she wants to spend time with it, learning to assimilate it into her self-understanding and growth; desiring to avoid sin, she wants to escape its reality, retreating to safer times when "such awful thoughts" were not the problem they are now. She finds herself a stranger in a strange land without maps or guides to direct her, and because in years past religious typically did not discuss sexual concerns, she feels that she is totally alone in her private sexual battle.

Some of the sisters surveyed, either through personal reflection or through information derived from workshops, reading, or discussion, were able to incorporate increased sexual desires into their total selves, understanding them to be a normal part of adult development. Others were not. Access to good information and honest discussion seemed to be the key to coping.

Not all sisters reporting increased sexual desires acted on them, but over half—69 percent—*did* engage in some form of physical/ affectionate behavior that they considered to be sexual. The most frequently reported age for involvement was, predictably, between thirty-five and forty, with many reporting involvement during the early thirties and early forties as well. Sisters' sexual behaviors ranged from prolonged embracing to genital intercourse. Some reported "one time only" experiences while others reported numerous encounters over prolonged periods. Of those who indicated sexual involvement, 97 percent reported "prolonged embracing"; 77 percent, "intentionally sexual kissing on the mouth"; 59 percent, "soul [French] kissing"; 60 percent, "petting/stroking"; 42 percent, "touching partner's genitals"; and 11 percent, "intercourse." Forty-nine percent of the religious indicated a male partner; 21 percent, a female; and 30 percent, both male and female partners.

These figures are apparently not chance statistics generated by an isolated research endeavor. While researching for her doctoral dissertation, Ellen Rufft, C.D.P., compared lay women and women religious between the ages of forty-six and fifty-five on their experiences of midlife transition. In questioning them about specifically sexual behaviors, Rufft discovered that 89 of 117 women religious had nonsexual relations with a male; 44 of 117 had sexual relations—excluding intercourse—with a male; and 4 of 117 had intercourse. Forty-one percent of the women religious Rufft polled reported involvement with a male and 39 percent reported involvement with a female.[26] Although the two studies cited did not ask identical questions, their similarities—both in content and results—suggest that midlife women religious do, in fact, engage in affectionate/sexual behaviors as part of their midlife sexual questioning.

It would be rash to assume that religious in their late thirties and early forties automatically, because of their age, are sexually active. The issue is much too complex to warrant simple conclusions. Several possible explantions and combinations of explanations can be suggested, however.

Some sisters engaged in sexual behaviors out of curiosity. Raised in an atmosphere of sexual denial which has now been challenged by contemporary psychological and theological insights, they questioned the "big deal" made out of sex and decided to find out for themselves what it was about.

I believe we must become aware of ourselves as sexual beings; I began sensing myself as a sexual being and felt a need to own that.
[age thirty-four]

I became sexually active because of the new sexual energies I felt, and I didn't know what was appropriate and inappropriate as I have *never* felt this way before. [age thirty-five]

I had a sense that I repressed adolescence and that it is okay to discover me as a woman and me as sexual. I have this recurring thought that *God is not* afraid of my sexuality, so I can relax with it a bit.
[age thirty-seven]

I feared to even be touched and even more to be kissed by someone outside my family. I felt like it was sinful for me. [age thirty-seven]

Women who entered community immediately after high school had few experiences with either dating or sexual play. Although such involvements need not constitute prerequisites for acceptance into religious life, the lack of exposure to developmentally appropriate "crushes," infatuations, and sexual exploration left many of them vulnerable to curiosity in their thirties, a period of increased sexual interests and desire. Some comments reflected this:

> A very young girl—me—made a decision that I would never engage in any form of sexual behavior. Now a much older woman—me—is wondering about the validity of that commitment. How could I say I would never do something when I didn't know what it was I was rejecting? I had to find out for myself; now I know, and am comfortable with my commitment to celibacy.   [age fifty]

> I realized that I was keeping a distance from others out of fear rather than conviction. That's no basis for celibacy! Until I learned that I did not need to fear my body, my sexuality, I was plagued by curiosity and doubt. I'm much happier now, and a much stronger celibate; I've made a decision *for* celibacy rather than a decision *against* sex.
> [age thirty-nine]

Whereas some experimented with sexual behaviors out of curiosity, others experimented with them to determine their place in affection and intimacy. The contemporary popular emphasis on sexuality in relationship provides few alternatives to persons who are unsure of their affectionate expressions, their sexuality, and the relationship of both to intimacy. Some sisters felt they had to risk determining this for themselves.

> Several years ago I met a minister; we were very close. He was meeting many of my needs for male companionship, and I thought some of our affectionate expressions were a necessary part of the relationship. After that, I met another man for whom I cared a great deal. Through this second relationship, I learned that the earlier sexuality was something I didn't really need as part of relationship.   [age forty-three]

> I think I have a greater understanding of the mystery of sex and an appreciation of this mystery in relationships because of my own confusing experiences—also I am less prone to condemn anyone for her problems.   [age forty-five]

I feel lucky that I was not "hurt" by my lack of experiences with a male friend which could have really caused problems. I have a sense of myself as having grown.   [age forty-seven]

Several reported sexual involvement as part of being infatuated by or loving another. Their responses to highly unique and special encounters included affectionate/sexual expressions which they accepted within the context of the relationship.

I experienced love; a person really loved *me* for *myself* and I needed that to grow maturely. I think God permitted me to fall into that for many reasons and it makes sense to me. It was a painful yet love-filled time and it *had* to happen to make *me* the *me* I am now—a *better* person on the whole than I was at thirty when I was determined to be a *saint*.   [age fifty-three]

My attitude sexually has changed from the romantic and incendiary to the deeply passionate. Why? I have met someone with whom I would like to share my life.   [age thirty-four]

Trite though it may sound, I fell in love. It's as simple as that.
          [age forty-four]

Regardless of the motivation for the relationships, the sexual behaviors reported by women religious were precipitated by their growing awareness of themselves as whole persons, including their sexual selves. No easy transition, it surfaced for many as a need for education, workshops, and discussions with others in order to arrive at a satisfactory understanding of sexuality in general and of personal sexual feelings and behaviors in particular. Religious are not immune to sociocultural pressures glamorizing sex, nor are they exempt from the emerging impact of humanistic psychology which urges acceptance and integration of the whole person. These forces, together with an enlightened scrutiny of the traditional teachings of the Church, challenge many midlife wanderers to reassess their former beliefs about sex and sexuality.

My attitude toward legislation changed. I began to rethink attitudes and behaviors.   [age forty-one]

I finally realized that sex was natural to humans and not bad—old religious taboos in some ways [were] untenable and ridiculous.

[age forty-four]

I realized that sex is normal, not wrong, and that entering religious life does not make these feelings cease.   [age forty-one]

I suspect many things [affected my attitude toward sexuality]. The women's movement, the so-called sexual revolution, my own "revolution," greater understanding of what the real moral issues are (and they aren't bedroom issues, either, even though the male celibate hierarchy thinks they are!), and obviously a greater sense of myself— including my body.   [age thirty-eight]

This discussion is intended to acknowledge and to help us understand the struggles and resolutions of midlife religious confronting intimacy/sexuality issues; it is not intended as a defense of sexual behaviors nor is it a checklist of do's and don't's to challenge the midlife wanderer. Each woman had to assess her own situation, had to reflect on her own confusions, and had to arrive at her own conclusions. Many experienced turmoil and joy, heartache and elation. The journey was seldom simple and painless, despite the freedom reported by those who have successfully weathered their midlife intimacy storms.

In resolving personal attitudes about sex, some women religious experienced considerable guilt. "I have stooped so low"; "What I did was sinful"; and "This is unacceptable behavior" were comments volunteered by a few. It seems that the majority of sisters engaging in sexual behaviors were able to cope best when they had the opportunity to discuss the issues openly with others, whether they be friends, counselors, or spiritual directors. Learning that they were not alone in their feelings and reactions, they were better able to confront the problems directly and come to more fully integrated conclusions about the place of sexuality in their lives.

The figures noted earlier indicate that 51 percent of women religious reporting sexual activities identified their partners as female or as both male and female. To understand the implications of this statistic, it is necessary to comprehend the context of religious life today.

First of all, infatuation and intimacy do not allow a "gender check" prior to onset. Women living closely together, daily sharing aspirations, successes, and disappointments, are bound to develop bonds of appreciation and love. That these bonds are periodically expressed physically is sometimes the natural result of openness and honesty. A forty-nine-year-old sister concluded her thoughts on the matter with her simple statement, "It was the people who came into my life that were important—not their sex."

Another sister, thirty-eight years old, explained her relationship this way:

> I am in an intimate relationship with another sister and have been for four years. The depth of sharing and communication is phenomenal—has been a tremendous growth and gift for us both. It has been the only constant during the "crisis" time. Affirmation and confrontation both are strong elements in our relationship which has expressed itself physically.

Discussing her same-sex relationship within the context of morality and personal decision-making, a forty-eight-year-old sister explained:

> Somehow I realized I could not have such a strong attraction to holiness and be committing only "mortal" sins. Tillich helped me understand sin as being in the singular—I never felt turned away from God. Later during infatuation leading toward real love I never felt "sexual." There was a desire to express love and human beings are somewhat limited as to how it can be expressed. I do not believe every homosexual act is homosexual—but determined by one's motives. How I express love does not bother me—what I express and why I express are extremly important—Harding's book, *The Way of All Women*, expresses my thoughts quite accurately; written in 1932, it is the best book out on women.

Second, some sisters who reported sexual involvement with other females indicated that their experiences had been singular events, unplanned, resulting spontaneously and unexpectedly after particularly moving or intense moments. Of course, many involved in heterosexual experiences reported the same thing. In both cases, the intensity of the moment and the impulse to express that intensity were paramount; the form that the expression took—sexual involvement—was secondary or even incidental.

Third, a few indicated that they had consciously chosen to become involved with women because of their commitment to the women's liberation movement, which presents a strong plea for mutual, loving, and even sexual support among women.

> I was struggling to figure out what my sexuality and celibacy meant to me at the same time [that] I was doing a lot of reading in women's liberation literature. I felt the only honest experimentation—for me—included another woman. [The forty-four-year-old religious who wrote this went on to explain that her experiences convinced her that she was a celibate heterosexual.]

Whether sexually active or not, whether heterosexual or not, the women religious who willingly discussed their sexual feelings and behaviors, especially those in their middle years, are actively seeking personal answers to their questions about sexuality and celibacy. Disgruntlement with traditional prohibitions that contain an implicit denigration of sex as well as "latent adolescent experimentation" (an expression used by several) have contributed to the present statistics. The extent to which active experimentation or sexual involvement or both will continue among religious is unknown, dependent, of course, on the ages and experiences of those currently seeking admission to religious life as well as emerging theologies and new understandings of the vow of celibacy. It is important to remember that all those quoted and counted in the preceding discussion are currently in religious life; had celibacy or sexuality issues been too enormous a burden for them, it is highly unlikely tht they would have been available to respond to the issue at all. These are women who value religious life and actively seek more effective philosophies for living that life to its fullest, incorporating an integrated adult sense of their human and spiritual selves.

> I was thirty-seven before my work with and friendship with a man brought me the experience of realizing I am actually "attractive" to men—a sense of my womanhoood which was richer and deeper than ever before. This was freeing for me. Since that time I have permitted myself to love and be loved deeply, secure in the self-awareness that I

am/will remain a celibate person. Because of this, I have the added richness of several male friends who are significant persons for me.

The comments of this forty-seven-year-old sister were repeated by another woman of the same age who concluded, "I have made definite choices about affectionate behavior I will engage in." For both, it seems that their experiences with affection and sexuality have intensified their understanding of and commitment to celibacy.

Another sister, thirty-seven years old, wrote the following:

> Personal experiences of love and intimacy have been the breakthrough for me. Intricately involved in that is also a deep commitment to truth and to growth on my part. I am excited about what is happening in me though it is hard and I often feel very vulnerable (like "scratch me and I'll cry"). I am fortunate in having both support persons and sound advisors. Love certainly *is* what life and Gospel and God are all about.

Another thirty-seven-year-old, reflecting on her sexual behaviors, decided, "I feel that God would not condemn me because I have loved too much."

Lest all this suggest that sexual experimentation is only a pleasant, enjoyable experience required for deepened commitment to religious life and celibacy, consider the following reflections offered by a thirty-eight-year-old religious:

> My sexual behavior is and has been different with each significant person. I have experienced deeply the sense of change from physical curiosity (at twenty-seven) to more intense physical relationship with my male friend I wanted to marry. Now my relationship with a priest is very deep, and though we would love the genital, we have agreed to remain celibate.
>
> When I was sexual with the person I thought I wanted to marry I always felt unhappy after sex. I know now that I really didn't love him.
>
> All these experiences have drawn me deeply into my love for God. I know I am loved and that I am loving! I was torn into pieces. I was torn between two goods—religious life and marriage. I was happy in community so it made it terrifically painful.

Women religious, like their lay sisters, experience increased sexual interest during their thirties and forties. Desiring intimacy, they suffer tremendous conflict trying to determine the extent to which intimacy and sexuality are interdependent. Often disenchanted with their work and their religious life-style, some turn to sexuality to alleviate loneliness and confusion. Others, brought up on traditional morality, reach a time in their lives when they feel compelled to formulate an adult commitment to celibacy and all that that commitment entails—including an awareness of themselves as sexual beings. The turbulence resulting from career/vocational upsets concomitant with searching for meaningful relationships during a very lonely period of adult development leads some to relationships with men, others to relationships with women, and still others to relationships with both. Each sister must resolve the celibacy dilemma according to her unique personality and moral standards; no single explanation for sexual behaviors among midlife religious can adequately account for all religious' experiences.

It is understandable that some people—men and women, religious and lay—respond to this information with horror and skepticism; they pray that it will pass away or be suppressed through denial and censure. Some, after hearing this information, asked that it be dropped from midlife workshops and seminars so that young women religious do not get ideas or so that lay people will not be scandalized. Such an ostrichlike approach to information might serve the interests of deniers and image-conscious persons, but it does little to meet the needs of contemporary religious struggling with the realities of intimacy, commitment, and celibacy. The midlife wanderer of today wants and needs information to help her emerge from her childlike protected status of the past to embrace her adult reality in the present.

Midlife workshop participants' reactions to this material have been overwhelmingly positive. "You've finally said the words"; "Thank you for asking us"; and "We appreciate your nonjudgmental approach" were phrases reiterated through numerous presentations.

A religious in her midfifties attending a midlife workshop with two of her housemates in their thirties returned from the "intimacy session" break tired but beaming. She and her sisters had stayed up half the night talking about their hopes, fears, and sexual behaviors for the first time since living together. "The tension is gone. Once we heard you say it all, we were finally ready to say it for ourselves. I understand them so much better now—and they, me."

Another sister, reflecting the comments of many, said that she mustered the courage to discuss her "secret sins and fears" with a friend following a presentation of this material. "I was so relieved to learn that I wasn't alone, and suddenly I knew I didn't have to hide it any longer."

These reactions suggest that honest confrontation of sexual fears and experiences with supportive religious who accept and understand the pain and confusions of interpersonal growth lead to meaningful bonding among sisters. They share hopes and sufferings— embracing while forgiving, loving while listening, learning while struggling. The midlife wanderer may often feel lonely, but she need not be alone.

---

1. Hugh Carter and Paul Glick, *Marriage and Divorce: A Social and Economic Study* (Cambridge, Mass.: Harvard University Press, 1970).
2. Kolbenschlag, *Kiss Sleeping Beauty Good-Bye.*
3. Georgia Dulles, "More Women Risk the Big Switch: Changing Careers in Midlife," *New York Times,* 11 July 1977.
4. Hurlock, *Developmental Psychology.*
5. Ibid.
6. Ibid., p. 362.
7. Benjamin Schlesinger, "Remarriage: An Inventory of Findings," *Family Coordinator* 17 (1968): 248-250.
8. Sheehy, *Passages.*
9. Levinson, *Seasons of a Man's Life.*
10. Isadore Barmash, "New Jobs for Old Hands," *New York Times,* 29 May 1977.
11. Sheehy, *Passages.*
12. Levinson, *Seasons of a Man's Life.* Also see Whitehead and Whitehead, *Christian Life Patterns,* especially chap. 5.
13. Levinson, *Seasons of a Man's Life.* The mentoring phenomenon is much more common for men than women, yet women religious—more than lay women—are likely to have experienced mentoring because of their career orientation as well as genuine interpersonal attraction disguised as "direction" or "professional interest." This will be discussed in the next few pages.

14. Ruffing, "Mother-Daughter Remnants," p. 49.
15. Ibid.
16. Kolbenschlag, *Kiss Sleeping Beauty Good-Bye*, especially chap. 1 in which she discusses the levels of moral development and their dependence upon personal actualization.
17. Maslow, *Toward a Psychology of Being*.
18. Thomas Tyrrell, *Urgent Longings* (Whitinsville, Mass.: Affirmation Books, 1980).
19. Thomas Tyrrell, "Intimacy, Asceticism, and Infatuation," *Studies in Formative Spirituality* 2 (1981): 99-110, p. 99.
20. James Nelson, "Between Two Gardens: Reflections on Spirituality and Sexuality," *Studies in Formative Spirituality* 2 (1981): 87-97.
21. Fried, *Middle-Age Crisis*.
22. Eric Pfeiffer, Adriaan Verwoerdt, and Glenn David, "Sexual Behavior in Middle Life," *American Journal of Psychiatry* 128 (1972): 1262-1267.
23. The material on sexual difficulties in midlife is taken from Hurlock, *Developmental Psychology*.
24. William Masters and Virginia Johnson, *Human Sexual Response* (Boston: Little, Brown, 1966).
25. Virginia O'Reilly, "Relations in the Middle Years," in Anna Polcino, ed., *Intimacy* (Whitinsville, Mass.: Affirmation Books, 1978), pp. 72-85.
26. Ellen Rufft, "Stages of Adult Development for Women Religious and Married Women" (Ph.D. diss., Virginia Commonwealth University, 1981). Detailed information included here was obtained through personal communication with the author.

Chapter 6

Waning enthusiasm:
Ennui in the midlife transition

While growing up, the woman religious, like her lay sisters, believed she was moving toward a vocation or career that she would thoroughly enjoy, one that would continually elicit unique talents and skills, thus fulfilling her dreams and aspirations to make a difference in the world while engaging in enjoyable, actualizing behaviors. This myth is shattered when she reaches her late thirties or early forties and realizes that, having spent almost twenty-five years dedicated to the work for which she prepared, she may never have achieved, or no longer sustains, the level of joy she once believed would be a lifetime yield. Her sense of well-being and integration is wrenched from her and she feels, as a thirty-nine-year-old religious lamented, "If I'm doing so well, then why don't I care?"

Sometimes the midlife wanderer concludes that a change in job or location will remedy her lethargy; she suspects a "shot in the arm" is somewhere just around the corner, and all she needs to do is take that extra step to find it. She is discouraged to discover, however, that she is struggling through something more complex than a stale routine.

> Somewhere in my mid-thirties I got tired of teaching, and felt that parish ministry would be more fulfilling. I received permission to return to school, loved my time there, and found a terrific job in a very progressive parish. It was everything I'd hoped for, and I was never more listless. Everything seemed to be a waste of time.
>
> [age forty-one]

The irrationality of the transitional experience of boredom is reflected in the following:

> I had just returned from one of the most exciting summers of my life; I had met new people and done many new things. I was in my early forties at the time. My living situation for the year was as close to ideal as possible—energetic, insightful sisters with whom I could share prayer, fun, and ideas. My work assignment was a dream-come-true, because I was teaching the subjects I enjoy most to students who really wanted to learn. For all practical purposes, I had it made. But I was miserable. Bored! I had no energy and no desire to do any thing. I'd sit on the back steps of the convent every day after school, stare into space, and feel BORED. Capital "B," capital "O," capital "R," capital "E," capital "D." BORED!   [age forty-eight]

Barbara Fried devotes an entire chapter of her book *The Middle-Age Crisis* to the topic of boredom.[1] She notes that many midlife adults complain of apathy, disinterest, lethargy, and disenchantment with so many life events previously found exciting and fulfilling. Entertainments that used to be sources of refreshment and rejuvenation become cold and empty; promotions, raises, and innovations on the job seem stale and meaningless. The midlifer feels and acts bored as a result of her distorted perception of time.

Because the midlife wanderer is not synchronized with time, experiencing it as foreshortened and moving too quickly, she is not sure that her efforts at change are worthwhile; she is not convinced that she will live long enough to reap the benefits of her endeavors. Time moves too quickly for self-actualization and too slowly for daily endurance of midlife tedium. Out of step with time (while believing that time is out of step with her), she is unable to generate the enthusiasm that characterized her earlier involvements. Fried points out that "as anyone knows who has ever spent restless hours waiting to hear good or bad news, this capacity depends on an inner peacefulness and an unselfconscious harmony between the flow of time and our subjective perception of that flow."[2] The midlife woman feels trapped in a web of sticky lethargy that precludes enjoyment of daily life and stymies her ability to find meaning in routine activities. Like so many other midlife transition symptoms, the lethargy seems to "just happen" beyond her control and most certainly without her invitation.

Fried notes that the boredom experienced during midlife transition is qualitatively distinct from the boredom associated with excitement or anticipation. Children waiting for Christmas or a birthday party, for example, complain of boredom the day before because they are impatient for the celebration. In this case, the boredom is of limited duration and will be alleviated by the introduction of the specific event. Midlife boredom, by contrast, is a more enduring, pervasive sense of meaninglessness, emptiness; it can last three months or longer and is not eliminated by a change in routine or the introduction of a new activity. Fried also notes that midlife boredom is not reported as a universal symptom of the midlife transition.

Only 27 percent of the women religious surveyed indicated feeling bored for three months or longer, although the most frequently reported age for the bout with boredom was between thirty-five and forty. That so few religious acknowledged an extended period of boredom in their lives appears to be the result of semantic imprecision. Many sisters reported that "boredom" to them means "not having enough to do," a situation quite foreign to women religious today, who labor under the occupational hazard of overextension. It is not surprising that so few reported the experience if they defined "boredom" in this way.

If boredom is defined as ennui, however, as an overriding feeling of lethargy resulting from meaninglessness and lack of enthusiasm for daily involvements, the majority of women religious would be able to relate to the experience. Many acknowledged having experienced months, even years, of such ennui as they continued with their overloaded schedules and multifaceted lives. For the woman religious midlife wanderer today: boredom—almost never! ennui—almost always!

Midlife ennui is a predictable outgrowth of the transition upset. Because the midlife wanderer is uncertain of her future, concerned about the shortness of her remaining days and unsettled in her sense of personal identity and interiorization, she finds it difficult to muster the emotional component that added color and enthusiasm to her younger years. Viewing innovation as useless, she is reluctant to begin anything new; experiencing routine as stale and purposeless, she cannot envision herself thus occupied for the rest of her life.

Midlife meaninglessness is not the kind of ennui or boredom about which one can "do" something. One sister, suffering the emptiness of midlife lethargy, announced to her housemates that she believed she was going crazy. Her housemates, trying to be helpful, suggested involvement—a class, a hobby, a vacation, some community service—to fill the vacuousness of her life. The midlife sister saw not only no relief in these misguided solutions, but she realized, more painfully, that her housemates could not comprehend her inability to act on their insights. Their mutual frustrations endured until the midlifer evolved through this transition.

Persons suffering from midlife ennui are not being deliberately depressed or maliciously morose. On the contrary, their inability to generate enthusiasm or to find meaning is a painful condition from which they would gladly emerge if they could. They might be difficult to live with; they know that others are uncomfortable around them. This awareness only deepens their sense of despair and lack of control.

Fried discusses two symptoms resulting from midlife ennui: immobility and reminiscence. Midlifers who feel stymied in their ambitions and enthusiasms seem unable to generate sufficient energy to perform more than the most basic tasks; they might be able to go to work, attend required functions, and participate in a marginal way in family or community activities, but they are unable to initiate new projects or to tap into the vigor required for recreational activities. In a way, they are too depressed to do anything about their depression and, as a result, are immobilized. They might sit for long periods of time staring into space. They want to do something and probably become cantankerous if others do not include them in activities; they are equally set about being unable to do anything and behave badly when others urge them to accept offers of sociability.

Often out of touch with the flow of time, midlifers are unable to find meaning in the now. To stave off the resulting despair, they weave unrealistic fantasies about the future and reminisce about the past. The middle and late adult remembers incidents of the past, but midlifers in transition place the reels of the past on automatic rerun.

Fantasies and memories are the vehicles through which the midlifer retains a grasp on reality, constants in her world now painfully disoriented and confused. One sister, aware of her continuous need to discuss the past, referred to pre-Vatican II memories as her personal "war stories."

The immobility, reminiscing, and ennui of the midlife transition appear to be the threads of three variants of "boredom" differentiated by Fried: stimulus boredom, substitute boredom, and alibi boredom. Comments from women religious attending midlife workshops encompass and, therefore, give credibility to the existence of all three.

Stimulus boredom can be of two types: understimulation and overstimulation. Having too little to do, too little to distract, too little to excite can lead to boredom; anyone who has attended a lecture delivered by a monotonic speaker in an overheated room has experienced this condition. Some religious experience periods of understimulation, especially when they have been in the same job for many years and no longer find in it any avenues of challenge. Although understimulation is periodically problematic for some, overstimulation, which occurs when too much happens too quickly, is more often a source of boredom to the midlife religious. According to available information, midlife religious complaining of boredom are generally responding to stimulus overload, for they are simultaneously administering institutions, attempting to implement quality community living, and working to enhance Christian actualization in their parishes, schools and hospitals. Such sensory and cognitive overload is often too much to process at once, so the individual protects herself by blocking out the bombardment of stimuli. "I'm bored" really translates to "This is too much for me to handle all at once." Those sisters who did not admit to a midlife boredom based on understimulation revealed that they barricaded their emotions against unceasing demands on their time and expertise.

Substitute boredom is a defense mechanism employed by persons who are fearful of or reluctant to express their true feelings in a situation. One religious complained bitterly about a sister with whom she had lived for several years—"She's the most boring person I've ever met!" Further probing disclosed that the "boring sister" was forever giving advice and suggesting a "better way" to do things, a behavior pattern that led to considerable annoyance in the complaining religious. What the religious *really* wanted to do, although she revealed it reluctantly, was to tell the "boring" woman to leave her alone—a sentiment that does not appear consistent with the traditional tenet of love and charity for all. The unacceptable reaction was too difficult for the religious to accept, so she resorted to the defense mechanism of substitute boredom rather than acknowledge her true feelings. It was less guilt-inducing for her to say, "She's boring," than to admit, "I'd like to tell her what I *really* think of her advice giving."

Women religious in midlife are especially prone to substitute boredom. Having lived in community for years, they have begun to see some of the warts that were not apparent when they opted for this group in the romantic myopia of youth. They find fault with community structures, prayer styles, personality differences, and administrative policies; they question their own integrity for aligning themselves with a group so fault-ridden. Many would like to express themselves freely, perhaps by confronting some of the more difficult community members or by openly criticizing various policies, but are fearful of what their behavior might generate. Rather than risk unknown and potentially disastrous consequences for their outspokenness, these midlifers are likely to retreat to the safety of substitute boredom, insisting that community is boring or prayers are boring or their sisters are boring—statements that relieve them of the burden of guilt for so-called uncharitable or hurtful sentiments. Boredom, although painful, is easier to cope with given the nature of their past training than are anger, hurt, guilt, or retaliation for real or imagined injustices.

Several midlife workshop participants, especially community administrators, expressed surprise at this information; they had been interpreting the midlife sisters' complaints of boredom as a lack of interest in the community and had, consequently, been encouraging them to get more involved in the hope that such involvement would regenerate interest. The consequences of such encouragement, especially for those employing substitute boredom, can be understandably disastrous. Community administrators who are themselves in midlife transition often experience painful ambivalence about their work and position, especially if they are suffering from substitute boredom.

Alibi boredom, like substitute boredom, is a psychological defense mechanism employed to forestall a potentially painful consequence. In particular, alibi boredom is invoked when fear of failure is present; it is easier to avoid a task by claiming it is boring than to attempt the task and fail. Midlife religious, perceiving a foreshortening of time juxtaposed with the tremendous demands of their work and communities, sense themselves as in a unique position to effect significant change in themselves and others. Because of their cumulative life experiences, however, they are also keenly aware that such change is never guaranteed; thus, they are reluctant to commit the prime of their lives to projects that might fail. Rather than risk the investment of time and energy, they reject such perceived gambles as boring. One sister, a very talented writer, was asked to write her community's history in narrative form for commercial sale. She refused the request, claiming that the mere thought of such a project was a "deadly bore." She admitted in private, however, that the real reason for her refusal was a fear that the book would not be good enough to be marketable.

Midlifers unable to generate enthusiasm in their lives are often trapped in the mire of ennui resulting from stimulus, substitute, or alibi boredom. Such ennui can stem from a reluctance to embark upon personal journeys of interiorization as well as from a genuine fear of an unknown future. Regardless of its source, the ennui is total, pervasive, insidious, and painful. It is not an emotion that can be exorcised through a given set of activities or a prescribed plan of involvement. "Doing something" will not rectify emotional disequilibrium nor will "going somewhere" restore enthusiasm. Only resolution of the midlife transition, with its task of interiorization, will initiate a personal integration of life, a meaning for being that will generate the zest and joy in living notably lacking during this time of introspection.

The symptoms of midlife ennui are quite similar to "burnout," and are sometimes misdiagnosed as such. Furthermore, it is more acceptable to many religious—in fact, honorable—to admit to burnout than boredom because of the recent popularity granted this condition in the secular press as well as in many religious journals. Burnout, characterized by lethargy, impatience, and feelings of emptiness and disenchantment, is the result of unmet needs and is frequently observed among persons in the service professions—as many religious are.[3] Although treatment for burnout is neither simple nor quick, it *is* predictable because of the nature of the disturbance. In other words, since burnout results from unmet needs, the suffering sister must assess her life and her need structure and make the necessary adjustments to assure fulfillment of those needs, restoring herself to completeness. Burnout is a condition about which something can be "done," whereas midlife ennui is a process that must be endured. Confusing the two, which is easy to do, may result in prolonged midlife discomfort, for one may become sidetracked in the delusion that ennui can be "fixed."

The disequilibrium of midlife transition can take many forms: ennui, boredom, illness, confusion, dissatisfaction. No one symptom is universal. Some sisters, 37 percent, indicated that they had experienced unhappiness or depression for three months or longer, most during the thirty-five-to-forty age range. This is not surprising in light of the fact that depression is anger turned inward,[4] and midlife wanderers are often very angry women. They are angry with themselves for aging, they are angry with community, which they believe has thwarted their ambitions, and they are angry with life for its inconsistencies and injustices. The anger is often a foreign and overwhelming emotion with which women in general are poorly prepared to cope, so rather than lash out indiscriminately at systems and institutions, many midlife women lash out at themselves—through anger manifested as depression.

Regardless of the terms used to describe the emotional turbulence of the midlife transition, the individual concerned knows she is uncomfortable, that something is not right in her life. She may be dissatisfied with her work; she may be disenchanted with community living; she might be feeling very lonely or she might be very much in love and not sure of what to do with her feelings. Whatever symptoms her unique passage manifests, she often feels that events are out of her control, that she needs professional assistance. That need was surfaced in some form by many sisters: "I wasn't sure what was going on, and I really thought I was going crazy." To obtain an objective reaction to highly subjective events, to establish sanity, or to explore more effective methods of coping with the turmoil of the transition, many midlifers turn to counseling or psychological services—some for the first time in their lives.

Over 70 percent of the women religious surveyed had wanted to enter counseling sometime during their lives, and the most frequently reported age for desiring such services was between thirty-five and forty-five. Over 80 percent of those who wanted counseling acted on their desire. That so many followed through on this could be attributed to (1) a greater acceptance of psychological services as a viable method for coping with difficulties; (2) a greater willingness on the part of individual women religious as well as their communities to invest in counseling; (3) the increasing popularity of counseling and psychological services in society in general. Whatever their reasons for doing so, it is evident that a significant majority of women religious are seeking counseling today, and that the most common age for doing so is during the midlife transition. Of course, it would be both dangerous and erroneous to assume that counseling, like any other aspect of midlife discussed so far, is an absolute requisite of the transitional period. As one sister complained, "Do I have to see a professional before anyone will believe that I'm suffering?" As in all things, if counseling helps a sister, she should use it; if it does not, she should find something else.

Whereas some religious find satisfaction through professional counseling, others seek answers through their personal educational efforts. Seventy-six percent of women religious reported attending a workshop or seminar that affected their lives significantly. Almost predictably, the majority of these women attended their "significant programs" when they were between the ages of thirty-five and forty-five. Said a thirty-nine-year-old, "I knew I was going through something, but wasn't sure what it was. A friend told me about a midlife program and *that* provided me with the answers I needed."

Not all sisters in midlife choose to attend midlife workshops to enhance their understanding of their troubles. Some of the religious polled benefited from prayer workshops, for example, centering prayer, yoga prayer, and so on, whereas others found satisfaction in journal workshops or general educational programs in their area of interest. The religious apparently were impressed with programs at the ages indicated because they were actually in search of answers, their questions generating a receptivity that allowed the information to affect them in a growth-inducing way.

Coping with death and aging, struggling through interiorization, adapting to new command positions, and adjusting to vocational and intimacy crises is difficult and painful work. Desiring a relief from their cognitive and emotional struggles, many midlife wanderers unconsciously employ the defense mechanisms of stimulus, substitute, and alibi boredom even though they are unable to name them as such. Meaninglessness, lethargy, emptiness, and exhaustion are typical symptoms of the pervasive ennui that envelops them during this time in their lives. Despite their finest efforts, they learn that they can "do" nothing to exoricse their demons; neither a new career nor a new vocation will "fix" them because their developing selves—which are responsible for the ennui—will accompany them into their new endeavors. The struggle is a process, not a disease, and midlife wanderers are marching to a strange drummer that even they themselves cannot name.

Alone and lonely, the midlife wanderer believes that she is the only one in the world who is suffering so intensely—that no one could possibly understand what she is going through. However, she senses that expressing her difficulties will enhance her resolution of them. To cope more effectively with their confusions, all religious claimed that they would talk with another person; they acknowledged communication as the vehicle of understanding. The most popular choice for a confidante was "best friend," followed by spiritual director, counselor, and psychologist, respectively. The type of listener preferred seemed to depend upon the individual's personal needs, perceptions, and interests.

To be able to express personal concerns to another is a major step toward resolution of those concerns; externalizing the pain, confusion, or distress allows greater clarification, an examination of thoughts and feelings in a more objective light. If she insists on resolving her dilemma personally and internally, the woman faces the risk of clouding the issue further by her own myopic vision, a perspective resulting from too close a proximity. Attempting to formulate and explain her insights in a manner lucid enough for another to understand, she must present one factor at a time in some comprehensible order, a difficult but helpful procedure that facilitates resolving the confusion. Discussing, sharing, thinking, and probing with another not only ensure a richer ultimate resolution of the midlife maze, they also promote bonding, an interpersonal interaction that alleviates the loneliness of the midlife wanderer.

---

1. Fried, *Middle-Age Crisis.* This book is the primary source for this chapter's material.
2. Ibid., p. 84.
3. James Gill, "Burnout: A Growing Threat in Ministry," *Human Development* 1, no. 2 (1980): 21-27.
4. Sheila Murphy, "But What Do I Do with My Anger?" *Sisters Today* 53 (1981): 225-231.

Chapter 7

Midlife emergence:
The wanderer returns

What benefit do these years of upset, mourning, confusion, anger, boredom, questioning, and the prolonged "dark night of the soul" produce? What growth evolves? Is there resurrection after the death?

Virtually unanswerable to sisters immersed in the troubled waters of midlife transition, these questions evoke soft smiles from those who have surfaced from the agitated waves. Feelings *do* become more pleasant, peace *does* return, and the ebb and flow of life normalizes as the disparate facets of personality are reintegrated to form a more complete, understanding, and understandable woman religious.

Reflecting on her various growth periods, particularly midlife, a fifty-three-year-old sister summarized her reactions with the following:

> God moves in many varied and wonderous ways.... Maturity is reached by ups and downs and while I'm glad there are more ups in my life than downs, I wouldn't trade the down times or regret them. They make me the me I am and I know God loves me as I am now and that gives me inner peace.

A thirty-eight-year-old religious, still enmeshed in her midlife transition but sensing her emergence from it, offered the following evaluation of her experiences:

> While I have had some painful moments in my last years, I am getting more comfortable with who I am and appreciate the struggles that

have made me me. As I'm getting older I panic less concerning my being human and weak.... I guess I'm getting more accepting of myself.

Sisters learning about midlife transition or entering into it undoubtedly feel overwhelmed by the number and intensity of related symptoms; they probably question the wisdom (or sanity!) of living long enough to endure such turmoil. To these women, a forty-year-old religious offered her optimistic conclusion:

> Overall, it has been a tremendous adventure. I have been touched by deep joys and deep sadnesses in my thirties and have grown tremendously. If the forties can top this, I will be delighted.

Women religious who acknowledged a deepening maturity and firmer self-integration also recognized the difficulties of their life passages, attributing much of their current growth to these past experiences. Never deliberately seeking intrapersonal disruption to arrive at this end, all appreciated the significance of the growth struggle in their total emergence. This appreciation is reflected in this fifty-year-old sister's remarks:

> The past five years have been the most painful of my life, but they are the most growthful. I had to come to the realization that, in spite of the love I feel for people—some especially so—my survival and growth do not depend upon any one person or circumstance. I had to let go of people, places and my own expectations to come to a new freedom. I had to change my way of perceiving the world. I believe happiness is in one's attitude, and I try to receive life as a gift. I'm glad I had to struggle because I am more alive and free than I ever dreamed I could be.

Several women religious asked if every person *has* to have a midlife transition, a question that seems to reflect a skepticism about the plethora of symptoms more than a rejection of the transition itself. Experiencing life events, whether they are grieving periods or growth periods, is part of the dynamics of human progress, of being in the process of becoming; failure to experience change indicates either a refusal to develop or an inability to recognize change when it occurs. All persons are challenged by change and transition in some form, but the unique experience of those transitions reflects the individual's specific coping style expressed through her personality.

To understand the inevitability of lifelong change it is necessary to clarify terms. A person does not "have" an adult transition in the same way that she "has" some money or "has" a disease or "has" friends, all of which suggest possession or acquisition; rather, she *experiences* growth and development as an intrinsic component of the ongoing evolution of her personality. Experiences become acquisitions in the past tense but remain elusively personal, idiosyncratic, internal, and unique in the present tense. The experience is the process leading to a repertoire of accumulated life events which in turn become the possessions of adult development. In this sense, an experience is not *had*; it is lived.

Living her life, each individual is qualitatively distinct from every other, and her unique process of adult emergence, especially the midlife transition, is ultimately her own. Since the commoness of human evolution implies more similarities than differences, documentation of identifiable trends characteristic of a specific transition is possible; no empirical validation, however, precludes the uniqueness of the individual experience.

As a highly personalized process, the midlife transition is as multifaceted as the woman living it; it is possible that some religious encounter every symptom described in the literature whereas others experience very few. If the question "Does every person *have* to have a midlife transition?" means, "Does every person have to undergo every condition talked about in these pages?" then the answer is a firm "No!"; if the question means, "Does every person undergo a unique developmental process characterized by questioning, mourning, interiorization, and integration sometime between the ages of thirty-five and forty-five?" then the answer is an unequivocal "Yes!" The commonality of adult development exists even if the personal experience of it varies. Religious who prefer high activity levels accompanied by little introspection or reflection might go through periods of uncertainty in their jobs or confusion over their roles in community without analyzing just why they are suddenly so dissatisfied with events that were previously pleasurable. Others who prefer to reflect on and analyze their daily involvements might plunge deeply into the tasks of grief work and individuation, *knowing* that they are doing so and aware that they are experiencing a life transition that is somehow different from anything encountered before.

"Is it possible to go through a midlife transition without knowing it?" The answer to this frequently asked question demands consideration of personality style more than empirical data. Some religious reflect extensively on their daily lives, constantly comparing and contrasting their various current reactions to those experienced in the past. The likelihood of recognizing some difference in their lives is probably greater for these religious than for those who are less inclined to regular introspective rumination. Those preferring to focus on life events rather than on their reactions to them might be uncomfortable or dissatisfied with their work, families, or friends without necessarily embarking on a concentrated resolution of existential polarities or mourning processes. As one religious summarized, "I knew that something was wrong—that I was somehow different—but beyond that I had no idea of what was happening. I thought I was unhappy because I wasn't meeting all my obligations or because I was sick or something."

Applying value judgments to qualitatively different experiences is dangerous. It is impossible to conclude that a sister who is poignantly aware of and able to name her midlife transition is a better person than one who is unable to put into words the whys and wherefores of her distress. The midlife journey is basically internal, and only the individual herself can assess the extent of her personal involvement. Some are more capable of introspection; some are less capable. Some are energized by personal reflection; others are not.

It is also impossible to conclude that those who are aware of going through a midlife transition while immersed in the throes of that process are guaranteed a more successful resolution of it than those who are unable to name their experience. Intellectual acuity and experiential prowess are very different skills! Possessing the ability to name an existential process can be a valuable tool leading to understanding and acceptance; however, it can also be a "cognitive escape hatch" through which a person avoids individual commitment and plain hard work!

The entire field of adult psychology, particularly as it applies to midlife transition, is a two-edged sword. On the positive side, results from these studies have shed light on a previously misunderstood predictable life event; people are now better informed and better able to cope with their interpersonal questions and interpersonal crises. On the negative side, burgeoning awareness of midlife symptoms and the concomitant vocabulary have generated an overfamiliarity that often leads to a blithe dismissal of both the symptoms and the phenomenon itself. When this occurs, the ability to put a name to midlife is no longer a helpful tool but rather a vicious bludgeon: "Oh, she's just in midlife crisis—she'll get over it!" or, "It's just a phase you're going through. Hang in there; things will get better!" Such examples of dismissal illustrate how a little knowledge goes a long way toward minimizing persons and their experiences. Treating midlife turmoil as if it were a case of the flu or a delayed adolescent emotionality is an unfortunate and dangerous consequence of recent research into adult development. The challenge is to establish a healthy balance between informed understanding and over- or under-reaction to life developmental tasks.

One sister asked, "Since I breezed through my adolescent identity crisis, and since I had no problem adjusting to my twenties and early thirties, can I expect a rather smooth time of it during the midlife transition?" Successful resolution of earlier developmental transitions does not guarantee successful resolution of later ones. The ability to adapt to developmental tasks is certainly facilitated by well-developed coping skills, and it is logical to assume that persons with strong coping skills will survive the midlife transition better than those with weak ones, but adaptation to transition is determined more by the balance of personal resources and deficits than by past experience.[1] Feeling in control of destiny, believing in positive outcomes, having a strong support system of friends and family, and being in good health all contribute to resources, while the lack of any of these contributes to deficits. The fluidity of these systems underpins the fact that earlier developmental successes do not inevitably lead to subsequent victories. Family members die or move, friends change, and personal perceptions vary; as the constellation of resources and deficits shifts, so do adaptation skills.

Growth is a continuous choice, a repeated "Yes" to the planned and unplanned evolution of life events. Anyone has the option of nongrowth and can deny the midlife transition, never experiencing any of the symptoms outlined in this book. Not to experience upsets, then, is not necessarily an indication of "fine coping skills" but might instead reflect a decision for nongrowth. Some persons do attempt a foreclosed resolution of their midlife transition. An Eriksonian term, foreclosure means that an individual, because of her need for security and closure, declares herself in "fine shape" and "over the crisis" when she has, in fact, not even begun to deal with her growth. Of course, such a decision has consequences. Because she has not permitted herself to live with ambiguity and ambivalence, because she has not experienced herself in the depths of her soul, the woman pronouncing foreclosure on her midlife transition is out of touch with herself and devoid of a personal reason for being. Zullo outlines some of the consequences:

> A foreclosed resolution to the crisis of limits is often manifest in my tendency to blame others or outside forces for my situation. There is little or no attempt to take ownership for my life because underneath the image of iron-clad certitude that I project is an overly dependent and fearful inner child. Foreclosed resolutions may be evidenced through excessive possessiveness of others or a tendency toward overwork and frantic activity.... Foreclosed resolutions are basically counterfeit solutions to the crisis of limits in that while they appear to be workable on the surface ultimately they short-circuit the process of growth and exact a heavier price later on in life.[2]

The symptoms outlined in this book are not intended to be a checklist of reactions to the midlife transition against which a woman religious can evaluate her personal experiences. She might be able to relate to all of the symptoms or to very few. Owning what is personally hers is the challenge of growth. If learning that others have been through what she is suffering helps even one woman to restore confidence in herself and her personal progress, then the book will have fulfilled its intended goals; if, however, this material becomes a source of guilt or a blueprint for acting out repressed feelings and desires, then it will have been misunderstood. The universality of adult transitions is always underscored by the uniqueness of the individuals experiencing them; to lose sight of individuality is to deny the qualitative differences in human growth and development. It is true that much of the literature on midlife is an exaggerated reaction to a glaring gap in the understanding of adulthood. Knowing that all pendulums eventually swing back to center, we may safely assume that the contemporary overemphasis on midlife symptoms (with all the inherent dangers already discussed) will soon evolve toward a more measured, in-depth understanding of that dynamic life process.

Women religious living with midlifers in transition questioned what they could do to help their distressed sisters. Unfortunately, no foolproof list of suggestions is available. It should be apparent from the material already covered that the midlife transition is not a disease about which something can be done; no activities, no pat phrases, no specific reactions can facilitate resolution of the internal turmoil. This situation is frustrating for the woman in transition as well as for those who must either live with or observe her. Ours is a "fix it" society that does not tolerate delayed gratification or sustained discomfort well; we have been raised under the influence of the medical model and assume that we can list our complaints, formulate diagnoses, and prescribe cures whether we are dealing with our physical health or a rattle in the car. We approach adult developmental discomforts in the same manner, wishing to hear the symptoms so that we can institute the proper procedures "prescribed" for instant eradication of the "disease."

As a process, the midlife transition requires time and space for its completion. Truncating the evolution of interiorization only stifles or frustrates its resolution, so pat answers or prescribed solutions are ultimately deleterious. The task for those observing midlife friends in transition is to provide a patient presence—an availability, concern, and willingness to assist without imposition or argumentation. As much as possible, women religious witnessing their sisters' discomfort should try to avoid arguing with them or attempting to assume responsibility for their friends' feelings and behaviors. The greatest gift one sister can give another during this painful time is self and space. This is admittedly more painful and demanding than any schedule or prescriptive activities could ever be because no definite end is evident—no solution is waiting around the corner. A precious commodity to all people but especially to women religious, time is the very gift religious can offer their sisters in midlife turmoil.

Community administrators, spiritual directors, counselors, and psychologists must also learn to appreciate the midlife transition as a process; if the helping person fails to be circumspect and insists on immediate solutions, more problems will surely result. The midlife religious who is complaining about sexual problems is not always best advised to leave community to pursue marriage, nor, if she is disgruntled with her current occupation, is she guaranteed satisfaction through a career change. Sorting through the various symptoms to identify the internalized identity difficulties is tedious and time-consuming, but it is necessary if the enabling leaders in community and society who work with women religious (or women and men in general) are to provide an atmosphere in which total growth and development can be effected. Too hasty a solution for the initial complaint will only further compound the discomfort of the woman in transition and lead to potentially greater difficulties if she is forced to grapple with problems resulting from being misunderstood. Some midlife sisters *do* need alternate prayer forms and the freedom to pursue them; others might *think* they need variety but really need to spend intensive time with one style before experimenting with others. Each religious is unique, living her special time in history through her special personality. Textbook answers to initial complaints or community policies that deny individual differences mitigate against full actualization of the individual. A forty-two-year-old sister described her frustration with a counselor who was insensitive to midlife as well as religious issues:

> I went to a counselor two years ago because I was having a terrible time. I was dissatisfied with community, in love with one of the men I worked with, and totally devoid of any prayer life. The counselor had worked quite a bit with others from my community, but I think he really failed with me. He kept encouraging me to leave the convent, insisting that I was obviously interested in marriage because of my dissatisfaction with community and my love of the man I mentioned. I'm glad I didn't follow through with him. I can see now in retrospect that I was going through something more than a vocation crisis. If I'd left, I'd probably be in a bigger mess today.

Community administrators often find themselves feeling quite ambivalent about their sisters in midlife transition because of the demands these women sometimes place on them. As leaders, administrators know—only too well!—their responsibilities for community/institutional maintenance and survival; at the same time, they want to be sensitive to the requests for actualization submitted by individual community members. When they encounter individuals demanding careers, interests, or avocations other than those espoused by the community, they feel torn and angry; they want to be sensitive to the individual, but they also want to balance the budget! Again, there are no easy answers to these problems, but administrators should be encouraged to share responsibility for their decision making with the person (or persons) involved in the decision. The need for honest, open dialogue is quite clear. The midlife wanderer desiring to investigate atypical employment should challenge administrators to assess their reasons for granting or denying permission for the adventure; she might be a prophetic voice to community direction. Administrators, for their part, must challenge the midlife wanderer to explore her requests and her own personal growth process in the light of total community actualization; they might be a stabilizing force in her otherwise chaotic inner existence. The give-and-take then becomes mutual challenge and exploration, mutual growth and development, which encourages both administrators and midlife wanderers alike to stretch to their limits. Without it, both parties are reduced to painful and unnecessary misunderstanding.

Finding it difficult to sustain personal equanimity when bombarded by a steady barrage of midlife emotionality, administrators and counselors might succumb to the temptation to provide instant answers or ready solutions. Needing and taking space for private reflection so that they do not lose their personal perspectives should certainly be a priority for those who work with midlife religious; offering instantaneous solutions to presenting problems (initial complaints) to avoid the discomfort of unpleasant emotional reactions does violence to the administrator or counselor as well as to the midlife religious herself. A fifty-six-year-old community administrator explained her own journey through learning to cope with midlife religious who were making demands on her:

I used to get quite upset with all the sisters who came to me requesting time away from their work for study. They all seemed in such a hurry—and became so upset when I tried to explain that we just didn't have the money for everyone to be studying at the same time. I used to get into arguments with them, and took it personally when they didn't understand or when they got angry. Now that I know something about midlife and the behaviors that go with it, I feel much better about my job in personnel.

She, like many others, tended to take too much responsibility for decision making and, consequently, took things too personally when she was unable to convince sisters of the wisdom (and necessity!) of her conclusion. Midlife religious may be unhappy with administrative decisions, and administrators may be unhappy with midlife religious' insistence and demands, yet neither should withdraw from the challenge of honest confrontation in the service of mutual understanding.

Questioning the efficacy of undergoing a midlife transition while in the supposed prime of their lives, several religious entertained the possibility of postponing the interiorization process until a time when they have more energy for pursuing it. These women were not interested in foreclosure—they did not want to avoid the growth process—but they *did* want to put it "on hold" if possible. A religious resisting midlife transition will still feel unsettled and undefined, and, if she succeeds in avoiding direct confrontation of the issues, will be faced with them later—and probably with greater vehemence—when she has fewer resources for coping because of aging friends and failing health. Unless she has encapsulated herself in a tomb of total inertia and unconsciousness—or unless she is deliberately opting for developmental foreclosure—the woman religious, like all persons, has a drive to grow mentally healthier and spiritually fuller. A prerequisite to this growth is interiorizaiton, which presses for fulfillment regardless of the individual's preferred life developmental schedule; interiorization can be forestalled but never eliminated without a conscious rejection of life and growth.

The actual duration of the midlife transition is unknown. Levinson suggests that it lasts, on an average, for four years but never fewer than two and never more than six.[3] Sammon, who has written about adult development in religious, agrees with Levinson;[4] Zullo, who has also written about adult development in religious, does not. Zullo maintains that the transition can last anywhere from a few months to several years.[5] Reflecting on their personal journeys, women religious agree more with Levinson and Sammon than Zullo; they take issue with Zullo, particularly in his "few months" estimate. Women religious do not report experiences shorter than two years' duration; on the average, they struggle with midlife transition issues for two to four years. Like all midlife questions, questions of duration have no absolute answers. Some sisters weather the storm quickly; some take much longer.

No one event is singularly responsible for precipitating the midlife transition; no one series of symptoms adequately describes the midlife transition for all religious. Each sister experiences her unique growth pattern according to her individual life cycle, personality style, support systems, insights, and visions. Trends and generalities can be identified, but the qualitative uniqueness of the experience remains elusive. Regardless of its onset, and regardless of its unique evolution, each midlife transition yields specific benefits to the woman religious who courageously accepts the challenge to actualize herself.

There are many rewards for the woman who embraces her midlife challenge. Her transition provides a time of personal integration. Selecting a vocation, pursuing a career, developing relationships, and employing talents are all activities of youth, the time of young adulthood, when the woman religious strives to establish her place in the world. Through these, she makes a statement about herself that she hopes will be pleasing to others; needing and wanting to fit in, she pursues others' "shoulds" and "oughts," hoping that correct behavior will generate acceptance. During her midlife transition, the woman challenges herself to assess her activities and behaviors to determine what they mean to her in her overall actualization. To integrate her various experiences into a meaningful whole, she formulates an identity based on past events, present insights, and future aspirations; to internalize her self-description, she reevaluates the litany of demands to which she subscribed for purposes of acceptance and decides, in freedom and responsibility, which "shoulds" and "oughts" are essential for her actualization and which are guidelines rather than requirements. Wrote a forty-six-year-old:

> All persons go through some very difficult times in their lives. This can be caused by a variety of reasons. But it is their opportunity to decide whether they want a life of activity *or* a deeper, more meaningful life where they know themselves better, have true friends, and God is real in their daily lives.

Through her integration work, the midlife wanderer develops a philosophy of life that encompasses her unique lived experience and her future vision. Until this time, she looked outside herself—to her church, her family, her community, and her work—for a definition of who she was and what she was about. Through midlife interiorization, she determines for herself what she is about and fashions an understanding of her existence that she can embrace as she anticipates the second half of her life. Confronting herself in her essential loneliness at the core of her being, facing her God and her ultimate meaning in life, she accepts her identity and her spirituality as completely her own. Rather than setting her apart from others, the development of an individualized philosophy of life bonds her even more closely to others who have also formulated theirs, for as each religious learns what it means to become most uniquely herself, she also learns that in her human individuality she is most like other persons.

Plunging into the difficult questions of purpose and aging, the midlife wanderer honestly assesses her strengths and weaknesses and sets reasonable goals based on them. In her youth, she believed that she had no faults and could accomplish anything; as she aged, she began to acknowledge weaknesses but persisted in her belief that she could overcome them with sufficient work and willpower. By her midlife transition, the woman religious accepts that she has both strengths and weaknesses, and though she is still committed to conquering her limitations, she understands that she carries them with her always. She does not complacently reject efforts to improve herself but realizes that her weaknesess have contributed as much to her identity as a person as have her strengths. She owns her demons and understands that exorcism is not effected through a single ritual; she learns to dance with her demons.

Dancing with demons is a very freeing experience! Prior to midlife, the woman religious expended considerable time and energy denying and fighting her inner foes, fearing them, and struggling to tame them. Through honest midlife assessment, she can name and know them for what they are, and thus play with them. No longer denying this intrinsic part of her identity, she incorporates her understanding of herself—both her positive and her negative virtues—into her future life planning as she employs her enriched self-knowledge for more practical goal setting, reactions, and adjustments. Two forty-one-year-old sisters wrote:

> My present concept of myself is of a woman growing, learning, and expanding in many ways. I feel comfortable with myself and know some of where I am is the result of pain, struggle, and inner conflict. But that's ok. I'm very grateful for the people who have helped me grow and learn.

> The experience [of adult development] is something beautiful for God and oneself—if you hang in when the going gets rough at times. I'm becoming a more whole, gracefilled, loving, caring, calm and peaceful person. But God is not done with me yet—and that is good.

The midlife transition allows the woman religious to embrace all of herself as a being in the process of becoming. So much of her youth was dedicated to shaping herself into an ideal, a finished product of perfection. She could not always comprehend the value of the journey itself, so to hasten her metamorphosis, she eagerly rejected those aspects of herself that violated her ideal, not realizing that by so doing she violated a growth dynamic. Through midlife interiorization, the woman religious learns that she participates in reality by evolving toward an ideal and that an essential component of that reality is imperfection seeking to correct itself. Recognizing imperfection suggests avenues toward real goals—suited not to a norm but to the person in search. It is acknowledging that the God-in-me and the God-in-you and the God-beyond-both is evolving, is weaving the tapestry of process and becoming. Prior to midlife, the woman religious espoused a world and life view that were static—the finished ideal; through the midlife struggles, she learns that the process of moving toward the ideal is in itself alive, vibrant, and worthwhile.

She chooses life, including the life that she is, complete with finished textures and workable flaws.

> Actually, this whole idea of "accepting myself" is a trauma rising from a culture which told me, erroneously, that some traits were "perfections," some "weaknesses" or "flaws." The material of our being *is* the material of our being. We should have been about the business of "doing with whatever we were" instead of chasing after qualities of "perfection." They were the qualities of a certain kind of person—but idealized—like so many other elements of any culture. I guess I'm glad I realize that—or no, *accept* that now, and leave the rat-race for perfection to those who need races.

These remarks from a forty-eight-year-old underscore an issue raised by many sisters: that the norms of perfection to which they aspired as young nuns were and are, primarily, male norms arising from male experience. "How can I overcome pride," asked a forty-year-old, "when I don't have any? That's a man's problem." Hubris, impure thoughts and actions, and uncontrolled appetites are sins—and problems—for men more than for women because men have the freedom to live such that they are tempted by these potential pitfalls. Since men were the primary authors of spiritual development books, it is not surprising that they based their spirituality on their experience; they identified what *they* had to conquer to attain salvation. Having little else to go on, women adopted men's goals as their own. Through self-definition resulting from interiority, midlife women learn that neither their experiences nor their goals are identical to men's; they fashion their own standards of perfection based on their unique experiences as women.

Personal acceptance generates inner peace. No longer struggling for instant elimination of imperfections, flaws, and limitations, especially those based on someone else's idea of perfection, the midlifer relaxes in the identity that is hers. She does not regret the activities and emotional involvements of her youth, realizing that they were essential for her actualization, but she also understands that she does not does not have to expend so much energy changing the world while emoting over her successes and failures. Reflecting on her past experiences, a fifty-four-year-old wrote:

I have grown much—I have mellowed considerably. I have profited from my early foolish actions (which were not foolish at the time). I look at the past as "hindsight is better than foresight." I do not carry any guilt feelings. Thank God!

As a result of inner peace, the midlife wanderer modifies her "messiah complex," ceases berating herself for her ups and downs, and adopts schedules and commitments that take into account both strengths and weaknesses utilized to advantage. All of this is not to suggest that she reclines on an easy chair of contentment to rock out the rest of her days. On the contrary, she returns to her life with even greater dedication and enthusiasm, but tempers them with more realistic demands and expectations.

Individuation leads to greater acceptance of life and others. From her cumulative experiences, the midlife wanderer learns that certain goals cannot be forced, that various projects cannot be rushed. As a result of her deepened sense of identity and personal responsibility, she is freer to let others be free. In her youth she wanted herself and others to conform to specific styles of doing and being; just as she can no longer hold herself to these externally imposed demands, she also accepts that she can no longer hold others to them either and allows each person to be responsible for his or her own development; the midlife religious knows that growth occurs with and through others, but not by them or because of them. "I've learned that I can't judge other people's behavior," concluded a fifty-two-year-old. After struggling through love-hate conflicts, the midlife wanderer is able to forgive others their faults:

I went through years of being angry with my parents because of the way they raised me. They're much older now, and even though I would have wanted things to be different, I understand they did the best they could. [age forty]

She learns to accept responsibility for herself and knows that others must accept responsibility for themselves. Said another:

I would really like it if we could all get along in our house because the tensions are sometimes too much. I used to think that I could make all of us understand one another, but I guess that's a little unrealistic! I can do my part, but I can't force the others if they aren't ready.

[age forty-eight]

In her youth, the woman religious demanded perfection of others and herself and became angry when she and others behaved differently—"Why don't they do something about her?" "Why do they allow that?" She believed she would never allow such transgressions if she were in charge and was critical of superiors and leaders who seemed unwilling or unable to insist on perfection for all. Having learned through midlife interiorization that the "they" out there converts to a "me" in here, she mellows in her demands. Her firsthand encounters with human limitation, suffering, and essential aloneness have led her to a greater appreciation of the process of growth.

Acceptance of process and self opens the door for intimacy, for relationships wherein both persons are deeply understood and deeply accepted. Intimacy, which *is* process, demands personal integration, something the midlife wanderer possesses because of her interiorization work. She now knows that intimacy is an imperative—not an option—for continued growth, the experience of God-on-earth as two persons, immersed in essential aloneness, strive to transcend themselves. Having determined the place of sexuality in her life, and having distinguished between sexuality and intimacy, the midlifer is freer to risk relationship. She is affectionate, intimate, and loving—and a very committed celibate—all at the same time.

Her self-determined identity as person, woman, and woman religious yields an appreciation for relationships, for what they can and cannot do. In youth, the midlifer sought quantity rather than quality. Many relationships, numerous acquaintances, and people to talk with were her goals; to be liked was paramount. In youth, relationships were sometimes conquests, sometimes salvations. Having learned that her identity resides within, the midlife wanderer frees herself from the bondage of identity and status borrowed from the persons with whom she associates and liberates herself to enjoy relationships for themselves. "In an intimate relationship, people accept responsibility for their own happiness and unhappiness; they neither expect another person to make them happy nor blame the other for their bad moods, frustrations, or problems."[6]

Inner peace, personal acceptance, realistic goal setting, and personal integration generate greater contemplative skills and rewards. Learning through her struggles that life can always be appreciated more deeply and lived more fully, the religious is freer to allow the wonder of life to unfold before her. She discovers that she cannot improve her prayer by storming the gates but by attending to the God-within, waiting to know what her God-within reveals and listening to hear what her God-within says. Frenetic importunings yield to contemplative appreciation.

I really am amused at the carrousels of prayer that I allowed myself to be caught up on. Of course, that's what I had to do; that's where I was. Now I know that prayer *happens* to me—seizes me anywhere I am, as for a moment my whole consciousness melds into a larger awareness of pure life.

Like Keen's "Lover and Fool," this forty-nine-year-old sister survived midlife upheaval, tried and abandoned rote prayer, and now celebrates creative contemplation. She may have worked at contemplation in her youth—most religious do—but now knows that she could not become a contemplative until she let go into divine madness.

Contemplation is relational as well as spiritual; this is why few women under forty can sustain it. By comparing growth in relationships to growth in prayer, it becomes evident that both are interdependent. The following chart summarizes sisters' comments pertaining to growth:

AGES	STYLE OF RELATIONSHIPS	STYLE OF PRAYER
20-30	Wanted many friends; wanted to be liked, accepted. Concerned about doing the right things at the right time.	Divine office, rosary. Tried very hard to be perfect at this. Wanted to pray right.
30-40	Fewer friends; more intense relationships of longer duration; realized that I did not like some people, nor they, me.	Prayer less rigid; tried many different things. Intense emotional highs less prevalent. Sometimes did not pray at all.

| 40+ | One or two intimate relationships. Mutual appreciation for the other. I realize how gifted I am to have these people in my life. | More contemplative stance; I wait for God to speak. I have learned to be quiet. |

As they developed the capacity for intimacy, sisters also developed their capacity for contemplation. Grace does, indeed, build on nature. Although more women over forty than under forty are contemplatives, age is no guarantee of this. Sisters over forty who report that it is important for them to have many friends and to be liked by everybody also report reliance on rote, correct, formal prayer. Chronologically middle-aged, these women are relationally and spiritually young adults. To reap the joys of contemplation requires intimacy—which, in turn, requires risk. As the midlife wanderer assumes the risk of intimacy through resolution of the attachment/separateness polarity, she opens herself to greater contemplative capacity.

The rewards of peace, integration, and contemplation do not preclude interest and activity in daily events nor do they preclude any further frustrations. Although life attitudes and personal identity are more integrated following the midlife transition, they are not such that the woman religious experiences uninterrupted bliss for her remaining years. The comments presented in this chapter must be taken within the context of the entire book; as such, the outcome of the transition *is* qualitatively more settled than the transition time itself. To assume that successful resolution of the transition heralds a moratorium on all future upsets and conflicts, however, would be naive. Many religious emerge from their transitional experiences involved in the same jobs they have always held, pursuing the same relationships they have always enjoyed, and delighting in the same hobbies they have always developed. Some persist in traditional prayer forms or continue to espouse long-held beliefs. The changes are not so much quantitative as they are qualitative, and even if nothing has changed in her external behaviors, the midlife wanderer who has resolved her transition *knows* that she is different—she senses a significant alteration in her identity and motivation. From a tremendous storehouse of cumulative life experiences she can draw wisdom and insight, and does not hesitate to do so. She has learned from personal successes and failures what she can honestly pursue in the time she has left.

Just as the inception of the midlife transition occurs gradually, slowly, and often beyond the immediate consciousness of the individual, so does its resolution. She gradually realizes that her good days outnumber the bad, that her pleasant feelings are more prevalent than the unpleasant ones. Enjoying an inner peace that pervades her activities and perceptions, she is aware that something significant has occurred; she is different but the same—more whole, yet still fragmented.

Growth is dynamic, ongoing, changing, and evolving. Adult life cycles, though relatively new in the study of human growth and development, are emerging as periods of continuous assessment and reevaluation. Perceptions change and deepen; behaviors intensify and diminish. Each step in the growth process is a learning experience effecting greater actualization of the midlife wanderer as she fashions her journey of becoming. Experiencing transition, suffering through insights, allowing change and evolution to occur are painful but necessary stages in the human growth process. The midlife transition, like all adult transitions, is a beautiful opportunity—a gift— through which deeper appreciation and richer insights of God-in-process emerge.

---

1. Nancy Schlossberg, "A Model for Analyzing Human Adaptation to Transition," *Counseling Psychologist* 9 (1981): 2-18.
2. Zullo, "Crisis of Limits," p. 14.
3. Levinson, *Seasons of a Man's Life.*
4. Sammon, "Life after Youth."
5. Zullo, "Crisis of Limits."
6. Sammon, "Life after Youth," p. 24.

Affirmation Books is an important part of the ministry of the House of Affirmation, International Therapeutic Center for Clergy and Religious, founded by Sr. Anna Polcino, M.D., F.A.P.A., and Fr. Thomas A. Kane, Ph.D., D.P.S. Income from the sale of Affirmation books and tapes is used to provide care for priests and religious suffering from emotional unrest.

The House of Affirmation provides a threefold program of service, education, and research. Among its services are five residential therapeutic communities and three counseling centers in the United States and one residential center in England. All centers provide nonresidential counseling.

The House of Affirmation Center for Education offers a variety of programs in ongoing Christian formation. It sponsors a leadership conference each year during the first week of February and a month-long Institute of Applied Psychotheology during July. More than forty clinical staff members conduct workshops and symposiums throughout the year.

For further information, write or call the administrative offices in Natick, Massachusetts:

> The House of Affirmation
> 109 Woodland Street
> Natick, Massachusetts 01760
> 617/651-3893